Dyslexia

A Practical Guide for Teachers

3rd Edition

Margaret Crombie

SEN Books

Dyslexia

A Practical Guide for Teachers
3rd Edition

ISBN: 978 1903842 16 4

Published in UK: 2018

SEN Books
618 Leeds Road
Outwood
Wakefield WF1 2LT
Tel/FAX: 01924 871697
www.senbooks.co.uk

Dyslexia

A Practical Guide for Teachers

Contents

===================================

**"Dyslexia is never the fault of the child,
but rather the responsibility of us who teach
to find methods that work for that child."
Maryanne Wolf**

===================================

Foreword

"I am delighted to write this foreword for Margaret Crombie's Dyslexia: A Practical Guide for Teachers. I clearly recall the publication of Margaret's first book for teachers in 1991 and I soon realised that this was a ground-breaking book in every way. It helped to break down barriers that had until then prevented the widespread acceptance of SpLD in the UK and furthermore it provided teachers with a clear and practical manual that would assist them in supporting children with SpLD, at a time when there was very little support available.

When Margaret's first book was published there were few if any comparable publications available and Margaret was responsible, through her book, for opening up this field and informing teachers about programmes, strategies and resources for children with SpLD. This undoubtedly led to more successful outcomes. I know from speaking to colleagues in the field at the time that Margaret's book was a seminal work in many ways.

I am therefore extremely delighted to have the opportunity to write this foreword for Margaret's current book. This publication substantially expands and updates the previous work. Margaret utilises her vast knowledge and experience to make this book an invaluable addition to the resources currently available for teachers.

The Practical Guide for Teachers is very practical and ready to use – it is essentially a hands-on book for the busy teacher and also provides deeper insights into dyslexia, what it is, why it can be problematic and what can be done about it. Margaret explains the terminology associated with dyslexia and importantly how dyslexia might be recognised in the classroom. I am heartened that again Margaret has focused on early identification. The section on 'initial observations that may indicate dyslexia' is a key component of the book and provides observational insights for teachers ranging from the nursery to the later stages of secondary.

Margaret also provides information on full diagnostic assessment and how classroom teachers can more readily understand this. The bulk of the book in fact focuses on teaching strategies that can be applied across the curriculum - reading, spelling, writing, memory strategies, handwriting, mathematics as well as other subjects such as PE and foreign language learning. I am also pleased to note that a section on motivation and a growth mind-set is included.

It is too easy for children with dyslexia to become demoralised by their challenges and struggles. Books such as Margaret's Practical Guide for Teachers will help to ensure that ideas, strategies and materials are available and ready to use in the classroom and therefore minimise the potential for demotivation and the accompanying negative feeling of learned helplessness. There are also appendices, rich with resource materials, which I am sure will be widely appreciated by readers.

Margaret, as a specialised learning support teacher working in a dedicated unit for children with dyslexia, was well equipped to write her first publication in 1991. Since then she has expanded her experiences considerably being a key player in teacher training, in the development of materials such as the Assessment Toolkit, consultant to dyslexia organizations and a key board member of the BDA Accreditation Board. We are fortunate Margaret has made time to write this edition using the vast range of experiences she has gained before and since the first book. The fruits of Margaret's experiences and skills are to be found in the pages of this new edition. I am more than happy to endorse this book and feel confident it will be widely welcomed by teachers and parents.

Well done Margaret – and I hope the book receives the success it deserves.

Gavin Reid

Dr. Gavin Reid
Vancouver, BC, Canada

Preface

My first book on Specific Learning Difficulties (Dyslexia) offered teachers a concise and easy reference in times when the Internet and knowledge of dyslexia was far less than it is now.

There are currently many resources available about literacy difficulties and dyslexia, some for teachers, some for health professionals, some aimed at head teachers and managers, others directed towards parents and some for young people themselves. Many of these resources are now available online, the intention being that they will be readily available at the click of a mouse or track pad. The printed copy however is 'making a comeback' and many people prefer having the benefits of a resource that is continuously available and not subject to a Wi-Fi signal or battery power.

This book aims to distil what is important about dyslexia into a reference book which is accessible to all – though it is intended mainly for those who work in, or are involved with, the education of children and young people with literacy difficulties – mainly for teachers and teaching assistants. It can be used as an introductory text for those who have a little knowledge and wish to increase it. Commonly used terms are explained and approaches considered for dealing with challenges and difficulties that are likely to be encountered. Acknowledging the vast sources of information that are available on the Internet, links are given - always with the caution that websites can 'go down' or cease to exist. The printed form however requires no such warnings.

No two people with dyslexia are the same so attempts have been made to cover a range of profiles and scenarios. Dyslexia often does not exist on its own and co-occurring difficulties are common. While accepting this, the book focuses mainly on literacy in its many forms. Alternative sources are available covering many of the other behavioural and social difficulties and differences encountered. Early intervention is key to minimising later difficulties so focus is given to the early years when screening and assessment are important for gaining recognition and support at a time when help can be given unobtrusively in a whole class or group situation. However it is never too late to acknowledge difficulties and differences and tackle dyslexia whenever it is recognised.

This book fully updates the information from my first book and takes account of recent research and the increasing body of knowledge and resources that are now available. It is hoped that readers will find the book useful in helping recognise the strengths and weaknesses that characterise dyslexia, but also as a useful starting point in building their own skills and knowledge in tackling the many challenges and opportunities presented. With appropriate recognition, teaching, support and understanding, the future of those with dyslexia should look positive for all concerned.

About the Author

Dr Margaret Crombie has spent a large part of the last thirty years of her life, professionally and personally involved in the study and practice of additional support needs in general and dyslexia in particular. She has been a teacher, tutor, dyslexia specialist, lecturer, researcher, manager and author, and now works in the field as a consultant.

Margaret has also gained a reputation as a knowledgeable speaker nationally and internationally. She is currently a member of the British Dyslexia Association Accreditation Board.

Margaret chaired the working group that developed the initial Addressing Dyslexia Toolkit, an online resource to empower teachers and young people themselves to adopt an inclusive approach to dealing with dyslexia and find ways to overcome difficulties and realise the individual strengths of young people (http://addressingdyslexia.org).

Through this book, Margaret hopes to dispel some of the myths that exist in the field, and encourage an approach which embodies the learning, research and practice developed over recent decades.

Acknowledgements

Grateful thanks to all my colleagues and students over the years who have shared their research, knowledge and benefits of their experience on dyslexia and wider additional support needs. They are all indirectly contributors to this volume through their willingness to share their expertise and extend the knowledge base - and to Dr Gavin Reid for sharing his knowledge so widely and for writing the foreword to the book.

And to my family who have increased my knowledge and understanding of many things – including literacy development and dyslexia. They continue to do so.

Terminology

While the term 'specific learning difficulties' was formerly the preferred term for professionals to use for the apparently unexpected literacy difficulties that some children and young people encountered when learning to read, spell and write, the word 'dyslexia' is now the common parlance. The term 'specific learning difficulties' will be explained further in the course of this Guide, but for now it is sufficient to state that dyslexia is about difficulties with literacy which are not readily explained by a lack of underlying ability.

The term 'specific learning difficulties' has come to mean difficulties that are wider than those of literacy and could cover many other areas such as Attention Deficit with Hyperactivity Disorder (ADHD) or Attention Deficit Disorder (ADD), social communication difficulties such as Asperger's Syndrome, specific difficulties with numeracy (Dyscalculia), specific difficulties with handwriting (Dysgraphia), specific difficulties with controlled movements (Dyspraxia) and many others. Terminology is varied, often disputed and can lack precision.

Dyslexia itself can be a controversial topic. This contentiousness is often originated through a lack of acceptance of the nature of dyslexia and whether or not the term should be used. This Guide proposes a willingness to accept the term as a beginning on which to negotiate and build understanding and an appropriate plan for the future support and wellbeing of the young person. What is important for parents and teachers is not academic arguments, but what we do as teachers to fully support and build the skills and confidence of our young people using their strengths as well as addressing their weaknesses.

The preferred term for professionals and others to use therefore is now 'dyslexia'. Though there are various understandings of the term, and many definitions including the ones I will present in this book, there is nonetheless a general understanding of the term that helps parents, teachers and others appreciate the type of difficulties concerned. The term 'dyslexia' particularly helps children and young people to understand their own difficulties and gives them a common language to discuss their strengths and weaknesses with others who have similar patterns of learning needs. The lack of a single profile or common assessment pattern does not nullify the use of the term 'dyslexia' nor does it render it redundant.

Throughout the book the pronouns 'he' and 'she' are used interchangeably. Though more boys than girls are identified as dyslexic, the principles, methods and approaches apply equally. When the term 'parent' or 'parents' is used, it is appropriate to read 'carer', 'carers' or simply the person or persons who have responsibility and look after the welfare of the individual young person.

How to Use this Guide

This Guide provides ideas for teachers and teaching assistants on how they can best help children and young people with literacy difficulties and dyslexia. Suggestions are given to enable teachers to identify signs of dyslexia and know what they can themselves do to offer support. Guidance is given on how, where and when to obtain appropriate advice and assistance. Most of the suggestions are not new. Rather this is an attempt to amalgamate some of the existing good practice into an easy-to-follow guide, and where possible extend some of the ideas or recommend appropriate source material.

Guidelines are given on assessment and on the various areas of the curriculum that may be affected by the difficulties. Suggestions are made at various points indicating material that may help the child with dyslexia. The Appendices contain details of such materials, publishers' names and/or where they may be obtained. No attempt has been made to produce a complete list of such resources as the amount of material is vast, new resource material is constantly coming on to the market and previous material goes out of print or becomes out-dated. Suggestions are therefore only a guide to the types of material available. Learners will inevitably differ in the degree to which they are affected by their difficulties and the approaches used will require to be adapted and tailored to individual strengths and how these can be used to help meet specific needs.

School and local authority provision for children with dyslexia will vary from area to area and each will have its own procedures for helping children and young people with dyslexia. Head teachers and managers will require to establish the level and type of support that is available to them from outside agencies and what must be provided by their own school staff.

Within the United Kingdom there are differences too in the actual legalities and terms used, e.g. in Scotland, a Co-ordinated Support Plan may be put in place for those who have additional needs as well as dyslexia, such as health or social needs. In England, an Education, Health and Care Plan (EHCP) may be relevant if a child's needs are severe or are not restricted to dyslexia. Though such differences are important, the focus of this book is on dyslexia and what can be done to alleviate or circumvent the difficulties presenting.

Key to success in supporting children and young people with additional support needs is the relationship that exists between home and school. It is important therefore that schools and teachers use language that parents and young people are comfortable with. The term 'dyslexia' is used freely throughout the book. 'Dyslexia' can provide a common point on which to base initial discussions of a young person's literacy difficulties. In time, assessment and responses to teaching will determine whether or not the terminology is appropriate. It will help if teachers and parents are prepared to share this common language as a basis for discussion so that the real needs of the young person are not determined solely by a label.

Chapter 1

The Nature of Specific Learning Difficulties and Dyslexia

It is very difficult to find one single definition of dyslexia that accurately describes the nature of the difficulties experienced as these vary considerably among those who experience dyslexia. We should not just consider the difficulties but also the talents and strengths as these will help determine future outcomes. Children and young people may experience learning difficulties for a variety of reasons and this is evident in their learning as seen in the classroom situation. Some learners are generally slow to learn across-the-board, and develop skills at a slower pace, never quite reaching the level of their peers. These learners could be said to have **general** learning difficulties.

For other learners however, the difficulties only apply in certain areas, particularly where processing symbolic language information is concerned. These children often puzzle teachers and parents or carers particularly when there is a very marked and apparent difference between their educational attainments and their overall ability level. These are the children to whom we would apply the term **specific learning difficulties**.

These specific difficulties are likely to affect areas such as perception, short-term and working memory, discrimination, motor co-ordination, sequencing, orientation and automaticity as well as ability to process phonological information. They manifest themselves in difficulty in learning to read, spell and produce written language work, and may also overlap into other areas of the curriculum, such as mathematics and physical education. Behaviour too may well be affected.

When the specific difficulties affect mainly literacy development, we use the term dyslexia. Other specific learning difficulties include Attention Deficit with Hyperactivity Disorder (ADHD) which affects behaviour and ability to control impulsive actions, Dysgraphia affecting principally handwriting and co-ordination of the fine motor movements required to produce legible controlled handwritten work and Asperger's Syndrome which affects social skills development. These are just a few examples of the kind of difficulties that can be termed **specific** rather than **general**. This book however focuses on specific learning difficulties that affect literacy development. Though there is often overlap among the areas affected, the term 'dyslexia' has been in use for several decades and is now common parlance.

When determining whether or not a young person has dyslexia, particular care needs to be taken if the individual speaks English as an additional language. There may be some aspects of literacy development, such as phonology, where seeming difficulties are the result of differences between languages.

Care needs to be taken not to exclude dyslexia from our thinking, but similarly not to conclude a young person is dyslexic from consideration of only some aspects of their profile. Better to give the youngster additional support in areas of weakness than to wait and see.

Because of the overlap between areas of developmental difficulties, it can be tricky to try to separate out the various problematic areas. However it is important to say that in all cases where the difficulties are specific there will also be areas of strength and ability. It must be noted that there is a wide spectrum of specific learning difficulties, and that these difficulties vary considerably between those affected mildly and the very severe cases. Individuals are also likely to exhibit different patterns of difficulties.

Assessment of dyslexia therefore must investigate all the areas likely to be affected and consider how these match the learner's potential ability level. We can then use the areas of strength and talent to develop the weaker areas. Through knowledge of individual learning needs gained by observation and assessment we can hope to meet the individual's needs within the classroom without too much variation and adaptation to the curriculum. The section on Assessment and What to Look for in the Results helps clarify why the term 'specific learning difficulties' is sometimes preferred.

Because difficulties vary significantly between individuals, some authorities choose to use the term 'difficulties of a dyslexic nature'. While the reasons for this are many and are understandable, this is often seen by parents as an avoidance technique – reluctance to reach a conclusion on whether or not dyslexia is present. It is therefore best to avoid this terminology. If it is felt that dyslexia is mild, then best to say this. We must consider the definition of dyslexia that we are using and consider the areas described in the definition. If the young person's profile fits that of the definition, then that child or young person can be described as 'dyslexic'.

How Common Is Dyslexia?

Dyslexia, like many other conditions, varies greatly in degree of severity. On the one hand, we have learners who have initial confusions over letters, sounds and sequencing, but who get over the problems by the time they are seven or eight, and thereafter only occasionally face any serious difficulties, usually over spelling, at later stages.

These minor problems can often be overcome by the use of a computer for word processing. On the other hand, we can have a young person who, despite the efforts of successive teachers, fails to learn to read completely and who is totally unable to tackle written work beyond the point of writing their name and even that may contain a sequencing error or reversal. In between, we inevitably have a range of severity of difficulties and a variety of patterns of learning.

> If we consider learners who are reading well below the standard of their peers with severe difficulties with written language work, then the proportion of children with dyslexia is around 3.5-4%. Considering those with more minor difficulties in reading and written work might place the figure as high as 10 - 15%. This means every teacher in every school will encounter difficulties that may be referred to as dyslexia in almost every class.

How Can We Recognise Dyslexia?

It is the responsibility of every class teacher to recognise the signs of dyslexia and to carry out, or arrange for, preliminary assessment. Just as for other learning difficulties, this should be carried out in cooperation with the school's Special Educational Needs Co-ordinator (SENCo) or Additional Support for Learning (ASL) Co-ordinator. Although not always directly involved, the Headteacher should be aware of young people with additional needs. Parents and carers must be involved whenever there is a concern that warrants action and need to know of any problems that are being encountered. In areas where there are peripatetic support for learning specialists, then valuable help can generally be obtained. When dyslexia is indicated, help in assessment and devising a suitable programme can be arranged, though class teachers will be the main source of appropriate teaching and support. Teachers should be aware of the help available in their school and local area so they can seek help at an appropriate stage.

If there is very little or no improvement after a few months of focused intervention aimed at ensuring the young person is able to cope at the level of their peers, then a more definitive assessment should be arranged. This can be done by a teacher with specialist knowledge or an educational psychologist (EP) though an EP may not be involved directly but offer advice to teaching staff. Though it is unlikely that a child with dyslexia in Scotland will require a Co-ordinated Support Plan, if there are other difficulties requiring other services such as Social Work or Health, then this will be a consideration. In England if difficulties are severe and have wider implications, then an Education, Health and Care (EHC) Plan will need to be considered. Class teachers should seek advice about the appropriateness of these from the school's SENCo or additional needs co-ordinator. This is generally done in conjunction with the school's educational psychologist and school management personnel.

The checklists on the following pages provide indicators of areas that may be affected by dyslexia. Information on hearing and eyesight tests should be available and these must be checked to ensure these are not problematic and/or exacerbating any existing concerns. Many of the points on the checklists occur in all children during the early years, at nursery or kindergarten and into primary schools. However teaching should target all areas of concern as early as possible when difficulties can be tackled in fun ways that are reassuring for the child and will help the whole class. If difficulties persist beyond the child's first year of formal schooling, then more detailed assessment is necessary to ensure the child's needs are met before they affect self-esteem and confidence.

Dyslexia may exist across the wide spectrum of intellectual ability. It is however, often the marked discrepancy between underlying ability as exhibited in verbal performance and visuospatial skills, and reading and written language abilities that leads the teacher to suspect dyslexia.

Even though the assessment of dyslexia is dependent on establishing difficulties relating to literacy development, and children do not generally develop reading and written language skills till they have been in school for some time, nonetheless there are early signs that can be detected prior to children starting school. Early intervention at the earliest opportunity should therefore be the aim, with young children embarking on games and activities designed to alleviate or eliminate future difficulties. It may be that dyslexia will emerge as a problem later, but we can then feel sure that all likely difficulties have been minimised, and skills are recognised. The checklists that follow will help identify possible areas for concern that can be tackled early without the need for labelling at this stage. There is further information later and some photocopiable material on Early Screening that you may find helpful in identifying children whom you might later consider to be dyslexic.

Initial Observations which may indicate Dyslexia
(N.B. A photocopiable checklist is provided on the CD).

Nursery/pre-school

- Difficulty in reciting a rhyme or playing rhyming games.
- Lack of awareness of alliteration – the slimy snake slithered slowly in the sandy soil
- Difficulty in maintaining rhythm – clapping games, dancing etc.
- Problems with sequential tasks – doing up buttons, putting on clothes.
- Difficulty in following and carrying out more than one instruction at a time.
- Possible clumsiness – for example, hopping or walking along a line - particularly if distracted or attempting another activity (saying a nursery rhyme, or silly song) – automaticity.
- Manual co-ordination, uncertainty over which hand to use – for example, throwing and catching a ball.
- Possible slow speech development.

- Word finding difficulties – knowing the word but being unable to access it from memory.

- Difficulty in repeating nonsense words, especially if there are two or more syllables.

- Balance tasks such as one-foot balance while repeating a rhyme or singing a song, or walking along a beam while doing a verbal task. Check if child can do each task separately first.

- Distractibility – can be for many reasons.

- Reaction speed slightly slower than peers.

- Visual and/or auditory perceptual difficulties and/or discrimination – for example, not noticing the difference between similar visual and/or auditory stimuli.

- Difficulty or slowness in automatising routine processes (doing two or more tasks simultaneously), for example, holding onto a conversation and fetching something.

- Family history of dyslexia or similar difficulties.

Most of these signs will be present in all pre-school children to some extent so it is important that we don't jump to conclusions too quickly. However with this word of caution, steps can be taken to develop and encourage skills and coping strategies without the necessity to formalise identification or labelling at this stage. Using a whole group activity with a games approach will avoid any stress so long as the tasks are presented in such a way that the child achieves some success. These approaches will benefit all children and ensure learners are not isolated or singled out as they might when the difficulties are being tackled later. Some suggestions as to the type of games that can be played in nursery or playgroup are given in the later sections.

At this stage, labelling and formal assessment are not appropriate, but teachers should be prepared to discuss difficulties with parents using the language which the parents wish. Where there is a clear family history of dyslexia, parents are likely to be anxious and will be reassured by knowing that teachers and assistants are aware of the family history and prepared to discuss possible areas of difficulty. Any concerns can be tackled in a constructive and fun way with their pre-school child. Parents are likely to want to be involved in supporting their child so advice too will be important.

Early primary

In language work

- Poor reading progress irrespective of the approach being used.

- Severe difficulty with spelling. Sometimes apparently bizarre spellings.

- Considerable confusion over simple punctuation and grammar.

- Confusion of letters similar in shape: for example, b/d/p/q; u/n; f/t; M/W.

- Omission or confusion of small words: the, a, so, to, of, from, for.

- Auditory perceptual/discrimination difficulties: e.g. difficulty in recognising where in words they are hearing specific sounds, not acknowledging the difference between letters and sounds.

- Badly or wrongly formed letters, difficulty in mastering the hand and arm movements required to produce clearly defined letters.

- Uncertainty about when and where to use lower and upper case letters.

- Reversals of letters and whole words: p/d/b/q; *was* for *saw*; *god* for *dog*.

- Confusion of similar sounding letters: p/b; d/t, v/f/th; short vowels.

- Substituting a word with a similar meaning but a different phonic pattern when reading – *kitten* for *cat*.

- Faulty auditory sequencing in reading and in the repetition of words: *permilinary* for *preliminary*; *emeny* for *enemy*; *pasghetti* for *spaghetti*.

- Foreshortening of words in written work: *permance* for *performance*; *intring* for *interesting*.

- Orally has difficulty in finding a name for an object.

- Difficulty in doing two or more things simultaneously, especially when one involves the use of language: for example, skip and recite a rhyme. (Ensure the child can do these separately before considering these together).

- Transposals: *sift* for *fist*.

- Fusion of letters in words: *ar* for *our*.

- Difficulty in remembering what day it is, birthdays, address or telephone number.

- Difficulty in mastering the sequence of days, hours, etc., for example, lack of awareness that Tuesday comes after Monday.

- Possible history of slow speech development.

- Difficulty in copying, often worse from a distance such as from a screen or interactive whiteboard.

- Difficulty or extreme tenseness in holding a pencil.

In other areas

- Family history of reading and spelling problems.

- Problems with simple mental arithmetic.

- Difficulty in sequencing: days of week, months of year, the alphabet, word order in a sentence, number bonds, multiplication tables.

- Confusion over directionality: left/right, up/down, to/past on clock or watch.
- Difficulty in remembering a short sequence: numbers, letters, instructions etc.
- Mixed laterality.
- Difficulty in understanding temporal sequential concepts such as yesterday/today/tomorrow.
- Emotionally upset when asked to read or write.

Often the class teacher senses intuitively that this is a 'puzzling, underachieving child'. The importance of this should not be overlooked.

It is suggested that in cases where a group of indicators are present (more than six) and these persist into the child's second year of school, the teacher should note the precise difficulties early in the first term. If dyslexia is severe, it may be obvious even earlier than this. Steps should be taken as soon as there are any concerns.

The class teacher should draw in any skilled help that is available both within the school and from the local area. As mentioned this will involve the SENCo or additional support teacher and head teacher. Advice and materials and sometimes co-operative teaching support may then be available. Records should be kept of the nature of the help given and the results observed. Parents too need to be involved and are a valuable source of additional help provided no stress is put upon the child. Encouragement from parents will help teachers maximise the efficiency of the support and intervention given. It is important therefore to establish and maintain a good rapport and easy communication between school and home.

If, six months later, there is little or no improvement in spite of co-operative efforts, then further more detailed assessment by the teacher will be necessary to establish more accurately the level of the child's needs and precise areas of difficulty alongside the strengths which will help the child cope and possibly overcome the difficulties.

At this point, some standardised assessment is likely to be needed – not for the purpose of comparing the child with their peers, but to establish if the child is falling significantly below the level that we would expect for their age. Rather than highlight an individual, and to avoid any unnecessary embarrassment, many of the items can be observed in group activities, profiles being kept to help with monitoring of progress.

It is helpful to involve parents in this process. Their insight and knowledge of their child will be helpful for teachers and reassuring for parents and will facilitate the whole process of early identification and support. Parental awareness of their child's interests and strengths can help teachers to identify the best ways to ensure progress and avoid unnecessary stress for all concerned.

Later stages

For a young person only identified as having difficulties that may be dyslexia at later stages (upper Primary and Secondary), the following checklist may be more appropriate. Again a group of indicators would suggest the need for further investigation.

- Underlying ability and comprehension seem to be at odds with performance in reading and written work.
- Failing completely at reading, or reading just adequately in the early stages, with ability insufficient to cope in upper primary and early secondary stages.
- Mechanics of reading weak, inserting or omitting words, guessing, ignoring phrasing and punctuation marks.
- Avoidance of reading whenever possible, not reading for pleasure.
- Failure to spell adequately to allow the reader to understand or to barely comprehend what is meant. Avoiding words that may seem difficult.
- Inconsistency in spelling, even of previously memorised words – maybe right at one point and wrong when word is reused in same document.
- On-going confusion over homophones – e.g. *there* and *their*.
- When writing, omission of letters or whole syllables, or addition of inappropriate ones.
- Poor use of grammar and syntax.
- Mispronunciation, misuse or inability to accurately retain words for verbal use.
- Misunderstanding due to inadequacy of reading ability – for example, reading *hysterical* for *historical*, in maths reading *of* for *from*.
- Difficulty in understanding sequences read aloud or in comprehending and following a series of directions.
- Difficulty in answering questions that rely on the interpretation of own written work.
- Difficulty remembering the sequential movement patterns necessary for accurate letter formation, resulting in poorly formed and disordered presentation.
- Difficulty in remembering words and phrases that are dictated.

Initially, the class teacher must confirm that the child has had an eyesight test and audiometric test of hearing recently to rule these out as possible causes of difficulty. However even if there is a hearing or eyesight problem, dyslexia should not be ruled out as there may be overlapping difficulties present. This should be checked with the child's medical records and if problems are suspected, may require the involvement of the school medical practitioner with the possibility of further referral to an eye specialist or audiometrician.

Concerns about eye sensitivity and problems such as Visual Stress (also known as Meares-Irlen Syndrome, Irlen Syndrome or Scotopic Sensitivity Syndrome; though these terms are no longer advised) should be considered if the child shows any signs of headaches, sore eyes, screwing up or frequent rubbing of eyes, fatigue, patching one eye with hand, skipping lines and omitting words or aversion to bright lights.

Visual Stress is a visual perceptual dysfunction that sometimes responds to support with tinted lenses and coloured overlays. It is not in itself a cause of dyslexia, but if reading can be made more comfortable, then it will enable progress of other interventions designed to accelerate learning. Other eye problems such as poor vergence control should also be investigated by a specialist if there is any doubt. A specialist can determine just what is required but often a series of exercises will be given to help develop muscular control.

All these problems require the child to be referred to a skilled eye specialist or equivalent health professional. Parents and carers will be involved throughout and will ensure that recommendations are carried out. Referral can be made through the school's clinical medical officer, community paediatrician or the general practitioner. Though any treatment given will not cure the dyslexia, it will ensure that eye problems, glue ear or other form of hearing loss do not aggravate difficulties unnecessarily.

Chapter 2
Getting Started With Dyslexia

While an eclectic approach is recommended, when considering support for children and young people with literacy difficulties that may or may not be dyslexia, certain principles are common to all. Motivation, attitude, awareness of learning styles, self-esteem and determination are all factors which must be considered. Consideration of these areas and the learners' responses will help us determine where our focus should lie. However, initially, and while investigation and early intervention are being put in place, it is important to ensure that we maximise the benefits which can be gained from ensuring appropriate teaching and support. This will help all children, whether dyslexic or not. Specific guidance is given at the relevant stages later in this book, but it is important at this point to think about common principles.

> The key to any and all intervention is to ensure we start
> as early as possible, thus preventing loss of self-esteem
> and fear of failure. Intervening early is likely to prevent
> emotional and behavioural difficulties later.

We do not expect young people to be able to tackle concepts that have not been taught so pacing the teaching will help build their confidence. Enjoyment and fun should be a part of all teaching, especially when overlearning and repetition are required. It will help if children are not segregated at the early stages where group teaching can be appropriate for a number of children. All channels of learning should be used – visual (diagrams, colour, show, model), auditory (story telling, listening), oral (saying, telling, presenting), kinaesthetic (do it, act it out, mime, dance, make shapes in the air, draw, paint), and tactile (trace, feel).

Progress must be monitored and recorded at every stage. A checklist is often the simplest way of doing this provided there is space for additional notes to keep track of the exact nature of strengths and difficulties. The checklist should also take account of distance travelled and milestones achieved along with details of the interventions made.

It needs to be checked that the child has mastered each step along the way before moving on or attempting to synthesise various skills. The child should not be allowed to develop a fear of failure. Children need to know what they are good at and the skills they can use to help their weaker areas. Their interests and preferences should be noted and used to promote and improve their learning.

Regular support and encouragement are vital in the classroom and communication with parents from an early stage will help ensure consistent support is provided between home and school. Paced teaching and support with appropriate reinforcement should start from where the child is at and proceed at a rate that will ensure learning is taking place.

EARLY SCREENING FOR SPECIFIC LEARNING DIFFICULTIES

While it is important to recognise if a learner has dyslexia and ensure appropriate help and support, it is also difficult in the early years for teachers to be sure that there are no other underlying factors which are causing problems for the child. These might for example be social problems in the home, health problems or just be a variation of the speed of development – an immature child, or a child who is young for the year group they are in. All children develop and progress at different rates and it is important in the early years that we don't write too much into a situation where a child is encountering some delay in the development of literacy skills when most of their peers seem to have acquired these. At these early stages (pre-primary and early primary school) a programme of early screening is likely to be beneficial in identifying those for whom there are concerns. Appropriate help and support can be put in place before children start to feel they are failing. Full assessment at this stage is likely to be both unnecessary and undesirable.

As far as possible, the child should be unaware of any lack of skill or ability and should not feel they are at fault. It is important to maintain enthusiasm for school and learning, and attempts at this early stage for standardised assessment should be resisted. A label at the early stages should not be necessary for the child to obtain the appropriate support and teaching. A group and whole class approach too will ensure there is no stigma attached at an early age. Not labelling children early however must not be seen as an excuse for avoidance of giving the support required.

At this stage too, it is important to consider all areas of concern, rather than focus purely on literacy factors. Screening at the nursery stage will ensure that children who are displaying indications of any areas of difficulty can have concerns tackled before they become problems. Research tells us that it is possible to recognise signs, and that early intervention is often better than later costly support. Those children who are borderline and have their needs met early may never require to have later specialist help and support and may never be labelled. Taking a closer look at children in their pre-school year can give useful information on which to base early intervention and extension work at a stage when a play approach can effectively ensure the appropriate provision.

Almost all children display some difficulties at some point or are slow to 'catch on' in some areas. This is quite normal, so it is important not to assume there is real problem too soon. Many learning difficulties appear on a continuum or spectrum so children can display mild characteristics or perhaps just a few of many possible indicative factors.

Though labelling will not be beneficial at this early stage it may be helpful to note if there are any clear patterns that may indicate specific learning difficulties. Play and group activities can be designed to help alleviate difficulties, help children develop coping strategies and avoid the child developing a fear of failure. Negative effects are then minimised. It is important too at this early stage to communicate with parents/carers to establish if there is a family history of difficulties, and to discuss how you can work in harmony to ensure appropriate activities are in place to promote and try to accelerate progress in a stress-free way.

The previous section contains indicators/checklists of factors to look out for if considering dyslexia – the topic of this book. However, in the nursery or early years of any school situation, it is best to consider the full range of possible factors that may cause concern and implement support accordingly. In this way, children showing signs of co-occurring difficulties such as dyspraxia along with dyslexia, perhaps exhibiting difficulties in phonology, memory and co-ordination, can be identified and have appropriate help in all areas.

At this stage a simple checklist is probably all that is required to flag up concerns. It is important to observe difficulties **within the current curriculum** and within the peer group to ensure no child feels pressure or loss of self-esteem. Appropriate help and support can then be devised within the curriculum.

Systematic working through the areas of the curriculum where a child might exhibit signs of specific difficulties is important. So for example in Listening and Talking, a child may have difficulties in following instructions; in tracking through the sequence of events in a story; in recognising rhythm and rhyme; and in identifying individual sounds. They may mix up words, sounds and/or letters; they may have difficulty in remembering what happened in a story; in retelling a simple story; in reproducing sounds or rhythm and rhyme; in 'catching on' to an alliterative game. They may have difficulty in finding the word for a familiar object; speech may lack fluency; articulation may make speech difficult to understand, etc. These are all possible early indications of dyslexia when taken together, but they are not a conclusive assessment. Additionally co-ordination may be poor; they may have difficulty in doing up buttons; in putting on shoes; in kicking and throwing a ball; in balancing on a beam; and in stacking Lego bricks, and so on. These are all factors that can readily be observed with appropriate response from early years staff who recognise possible signs of both dyslexia and dyspraxia. It is the child's response to their interventions at this stage that will determine whether the child will require full diagnostic assessment and targeted and personalised support later.

It is recognised that intervention at this stage is much more likely to gain a positive outcome than a 'wait and see' approach. Early literacy provides the foundation for lifelong learning so it is vitally important that staff recognise the value of intervention to prevent long-term negative effects.

The child should feel they are gaining positive personal achievement from their experiences. Children will have different experiences dependent on the nursery or school they attend and the local authority provision that is place in their area, but wherever they are, it is possible to observe the child's responses within the curriculum, thus not adding to the workload of the teacher or early years' workers.

A checklist is available on the CD and strategies and approaches to support children exhibiting concerns in specific areas are given throughout this book. If a child makes very little progress from the early years approaches through play and multisensory activities then early years staff or early primary school teachers will require to continue delivering appropriate help while following the Route to Assessment (page 30). They will gain more detailed information on the child's level of cognitive functioning and any specific areas that will require a personalised programme of targeted intervention focusing on phonics and reading. Children who do not have adequate knowledge of phonics and decoding skills to fall back on will be limited in the progress they make in reading with subsequent risk of increasing deterioration in their self-esteem and motivation.

If a child does not make clear progress through following a programme of intervention then it will be appropriate to complete some more detailed assessment to clarify the exact nature and extent of the difficulties. It is important to ensure that strengths and talents are also identified and promoted. These can be used to assist in the teaching and learning programme with positive approaches designed to maintain the child's motivation, accelerate their learning and enable them to develop appropriate learning strategies.

While not all parents/carers or children will find a full diagnostic assessment either necessary or desirable at this stage, it is important to discuss appropriate approaches and future plans to ensure everyone is kept fully informed. Concerns should be discussed and recorded at this stage. A suitable format for recording meetings and outcomes is included on the CD. Documenting the current situation and agreeing future plans ensures common understanding and ensures consistency even if there are staff changes.

What is vital to remember in the early years is that a 'wait and see' approach is not appropriate. With or without a label, it is essential that children who are experiencing difficulties receive the right level and type of support before they start to feel they are failing, before they develop emotional problems, and before behaviour begins to deteriorate or the child withdraws. The children can later be seen as behaviour problems if the real difficulties are not addressed. Frustration on the part of the child can cause various types of response, but none of these is likely to be positive. Recognition at an early stage therefore is absolutely vital if the child is to maintain a positive outlook and parents are to understand why their child is struggling. They can then facilitate appropriate help and support class teachers in implementing the type of intervention necessary.

It is important therefore that schools have a clear route for teachers to follow if signs of difficulty become apparent and do not readily respond to intervention in the early years. Through acknowledging difficulties early and ensuring appropriate focused teaching and support we can ensure a happier, more confident individual. If children are assessed as dyslexic at a later stage then the understanding gained through following through the stages of identification with on-going support will ensure children understand what dyslexia is and how it is affecting their learning.

Parents know their children and it is important that they are involved at all stages of identification and assessment. Intervention works best when teachers, school managers and parents are working in harmony and any specialists are aware of school policies and procedures for working with dyslexia.

While the checklists that are on the CD can be used for screening it would be better if they were used as a base for a checklist specifically targeted around the individual school's curriculum. This should contain the factors noted in the given checklist but may additionally contain other factors that may indicate other specific differences presented in the context of the particular culture and content of the school curriculum. For example, a curriculum target for the early years might be to be able to hear and generate rhyming patterns in words. Difficulty in this area would be one indicator of dyslexia. Difficulties in other areas, such as co-ordination, may indicate dyspraxia. We would look for a pattern of indicators of difficulty in an area before deciding that further assessment was necessary.

EARLY INTERVENTION

Early screening is a first step towards effectively dealing with dyslexia at an appropriate stage, and often before the term 'dyslexia' can reliably be used. Early screening as we have recognised must be for all difficulties and also for the very able. As this book is about dyslexia, the following section gives suggestions for children who are recognised to have early signs of dyslexia though that is not to underplay the necessity to deal with all areas of difficulty as early as possible.

There are several areas where there may be difficulties which will affect progress in literacy development, and it is important to consider these systematically and even though there is no label of dyslexia at the early stages, a fun approach to learning will benefit a significant number of children. The following section contains some suggestions that may be helpful.

Phonology and areas of phonemic awareness:

Phonology is about the sound system of a language and the way in which sounds function within a given language. Though phonology includes the study of sign language, it is more generally considered to be about how sounds interact in a structured way to convey linguistic meaning. As such it is an important area that should be taken into account when considering dyslexia.

Children with dyslexia may perceive sounds differently or may lack awareness of the specific sounds or phonemes that they are hearing. They may be unable to pick up just how sounds relate to one another, and then have difficulty in relating the sounds to the letters that represent them.

Playing with sounds in the early years

Guess the word

In this game, children blend letters to form words. Firstly choose a theme – e.g. pets – say the sounds of a simple word (e.g. cat). Say the sounds slowly in an exaggerated voice (/k/-/ă/-/t/). "Can you guess what word does that make?" As the child 'gets the hang of' the game, gradually introduce longer and more complex words (e.g. elephant saying it as /ĕ/-/l/-/ĕ/-/f/-/ă/-/n/-/t/), goldfish saying it as /g/-/ō/-/l/-/d/-/f/-/ĭ/-/sh/). Ensure that you say units of sound as they are - /sh/ as one sound - as the game is about sounds and not spellings. The child of course will not really be guessing, but it makes for a better game if they think that is what they are doing.

Another version of this game is to **eliminate a sound** and encourage children to say what the missing sound is, so if we take the same theme of pets, then we can say /d/-/ŏ/- - what comes next? We may need initially to give some scaffolding for the child to find the answer, so we might say, "The lady took her /d/-/ŏ/- - for a walk. Tell me the word. What letter was missing?" And later when the child understands what is required, we can use progressively harder tasks with missing sounds in different parts of the word, building up to for example, /t/-/ŏ/-/r/--/?/--/oy/-/z/. "A /t/-/ŏ/-/r/--/?/--/oy/-/z/ can only move slowly. What is missing? What is the missing sound?"

The child can then **become teacher** and eliminate a sound and get the other children to 'guess' the sound.

Sing along

The teacher starts and child finds a word to rhyme:

Old MacDonald had a cow, ee-i-ee-i-o,
Old MacDonald had a sow, ee-i-ee-i-o,
Old MacDonald had a row, ………

Old MacDonald had a pet, ee-i-ee-i-o.
Old MacDonald had a bet, ee-i-ee-i-o.
Old MacDonald had a jet, ee-i-ee-i-o.
Old MacDonald had a vet……. and so on.

Keep it going with teacher changing the first word when the rhyming words seem to run out. Don't be too strict about the words being real words. If they rhyme it's fine.

I spy with my little eye and I hear with my little ear

The teacher says, " I hear with my little ear, something beginning with /b/. Child thinks of lots of items beginning with the letter – e.g. bang, band, Bert, banjo, bongs, …….

You can also use alphabet cards as you give the sound of a letter so the child associates the sound and the letter. Using the alphabet cards a child chooses a letter and says the sound. As the child starts to learn the written letters this helps reinforce letter recognition.

Tying the sounds with a letter character as we do in Letterland helps give further support. However don't use too many or different associations as this in itself can be confusing. If you associate Sammy Snake with the letter 's', then it is probably best to keep this one character to represent the letter.

Alliteration

Start by illustrating to the children what you are looking for – "Listen – Silly, Sally Snake Slithered Slowly – what can I say next? Hopefully you get something like "Silently or Sadly. You might even get something like 'circling' which would be quite acceptable as we're looking at sounds, not spellings.

Give a few examples like this so children get the idea. Then start to play games.

I went to the shop and bought – a pen
I went to the shop and bought – a pen and a pea
I went to the shop and bought – a pen, a pea and a pencil
I went to the shop and bought – a pen, a pea, a pencil and a pot
I went to the shop and bought - a pen, a pea, a pencil, a pot and a pan ………

Or the children can add adjectives

> I went to the shop and bought – a picture
> I went to the shop and bought – a pretty picture
> I went to the shop and bought – a pretty paper picture
> I went to the shop and bought – a pretty pale paper picture.

Done in this way, these activities also help memory. However if we want them to be as simple as possible, then we might just stick to getting one word beginning with the appropriate sound, and not insist in repeating the previously mentioned items. The activities are best done in a small group where the teacher or assistant can monitor which children are having trouble and which are coping well.

Children each say their name – for example, **Emma**, then the group help her make up an alliterative sentence – **E**mma **e**xpects **e**lephants **e**arly **e**xcept **E**ddie's **e**nded **e**lectric **e**lements. The sentences don't have to make sense or be grammatically correct. They can contain silly words and make silly sentences that all the children can enjoy. They must just contain the sounds we are attempting to alliterate. These are short activities that should be engaged in for no more than a few minutes at a time so they remain fun.

Ensure children are **focused** at the start of the activity and check how long their focus lasts. This helps the teacher be aware of the children's usual concentration span and how long it takes before they 'switch off'. In the early years of school, children who have a short span of concentration can lose a lot of learning. If they are quiet and cause no trouble, then often the teacher (especially in a large class) can be unaware they are no longer focusing.

Memory tasks

Check if children know their **address** and **phone number** if they have one. This can be done in the context of a story about getting lost, perhaps, and being asked by a policeman or lady where they stay. Do check if they get it right as often if children are dyslexic, numbers get muddled, two-one-eight can become two-eight-one, so note what they say and check later.

It is good also to be aware of how many **instructions** a child can hold in **memory** and follow, so do check this when children are working in the classroom and attempt to expand the number.
If at the start, the child can follow only two instructions – for example;

> "Go to the number table and get me the ruler",
> then challenge them to remember three items;
> "Go to the number table and get a ruler and then give it to Jack."

If they can remember three instructions, stretch it to four. Ensure children focus and get them to repeat the instruction before attempting to complete the task. This will get them into the habit of listening, saying the instruction back to themselves, before carrying it out. That way, it is more likely they will remember.

Visual factors

Though there is evidence that children with dyslexia have phonological difficulties and that is an area we must target, we must not ignore the visual. Children should be encouraged to give **visual attention** to particular features of pictures, words, word shapes, differences between letters and different shapes by asking in what ways things are the same and what ways different. Again a games approach to visual skill development is useful and the more we can integrate the visual with the auditory and oral the better the outcome is likely to be. Games such as Kim's Game where children have 60 seconds to remember a tray of objects or pictures help children use their visual memory, but it does help if teachers suggest strategies to help the children – such as grouping items, chunking, thinking of items beginning with specific sounds, letters, colours etc.

'**Find the difference**' games with pictures that are very similar or shapes encourage the focus of attention and training to use the eyes carefully to scan the page or picture. Children will require good visual tracking skills to follow print so anything that we can do to improve ability to carefully focus and move the eyes is going to benefit the children's tracking for reading. However if we spot a problem with this, then it would be best to involve a specialist orthoptist at an early stage to check that the eyes are working as they should for the age of the child. (See separate information on Visual Stress on page 148).

Physical skill development too can be enhanced by literacy activities that involve movement, so throw and catch a ball while at the same time repeating something we wish the children to remember – days of the week, months of the year, the alphabet, counting etc. We may need to do this very slowly at first then challenge the children to speed up. Again this activity is best done in a small group and where there is space, so it will be a good activity for outdoors.

Children can stand in a circle and say the name of the next month or whatever with the teacher going around the circle and each child taking a turn. With slightly older children we might use this activity for multiplication tables, counting on in twos, fives etc.

Effective interventions for literacy should be as multisensory as we can make them and include activities involving phonology – knowledge of letter sounds and names, phoneme awareness and early writing skills to associate letters to sounds.

Early reading must be at an appropriate interest and reading level focusing on enjoyment and success. Children with weak vocabulary must have lots of activities that target extending their vocabulary.

An effective intervention programme should last for a few months with regular and on-going monitoring of progress. This early intervention for a whole group of children will have been worthwhile though it may still require that further interventions be embarked upon. A lack of acceleration in progress will be disappointing but this does not mean the teacher has done anything wrong. It is indicative that further monitoring leading towards more detailed assessment is required.

More detailed assessment to identify gaps in the child's knowledge will help teachers plan the way forward. This may be gaps in phonological awareness, phonics, number skills, morphology or similar.

More targeted interventions can then be brought in to fill the gaps and build the child's confidence. At this point the SENCo or Additional Support Needs Co-ordinator for the school should be able to offer further advice and should work with the class teacher to try to accelerate progress. The head teacher should be kept involved and may call a meeting with parents to ensure they are aware of difficulties, what the school is doing, and how they can help at home. Further assessment will establish a base point from which to measure progress and target any new interventions.

If progress is good, then it is likely that a decision will be made to continue the current programme and continue to monitor progress. If however progress is slow or weak, a full diagnostic assessment may be required. An individualised educational programme (IEP) may also be desirable if severe difficulties are hampering progress and a need for additional individualised support and resources is established. There is more information on this on pages 53 to 55.

THE ROUTE TO ASSESSMENT

CLASS TEACHER
SUPPORT ASSISTANT
Preliminary observations and screening

Appropriate teaching and
support is put in place
to accelerate progress
in identified areas

SENCO or **ADDITIONAL SUPPORT NEEDS CO-ORDINATOR**
and **HEADTEACHER** in liaison with **CLASS TEACHER**
More detailed assessment and monitoring

Response to detailed assessment
of needs: continue with focused teaching
and support with additional teaching
strategies and ICT when appropriate.
Involve parents so that support
is given at home, too.

PARENTS/CARERS
involved throughout

ASSESSMENT
Full assessment
AREA/SCHOOL SPECIALIST TEACHER
and/or **EDUCATIONAL PSYCHOLOGIST**

Dyslexia identified.
If appropriate detailed
(possibly individualised)
planning and support put in
place according to profile
of strengths and difficulties

SEVERE DIFFICULTIES

MILD DIFFICULTIES

CONSIDERATION for
SPECIALIST SUPPORT

ADVICE from
SPECIALIST TEACHER
on ways to support

Chapter 3

Defining Dyslexia

There are many and varied definitions of dyslexia. Definitions also change over time and are influenced by research. While many may feel they know what dyslexia is and that there is no need to give a definition, this is entirely wrong.

**If we're not absolutely clear about what dyslexia is,
then when we assess for dyslexia,
we can't be clear what we are assessing.**

We must therefore ensure we don't just know what dyslexia is, but that we can evidence through the assessment process that a person has dyslexia or not. How we define dyslexia determines what we must assess. If dyslexia is defined as a word reading difficulty then we must assess word reading skills before we can be sure dyslexia is present. However, I believe we should assess much more than what is in the definition, as we'll want to ensure we have a complete profile of the individual's needs in order to meet their specific requirements. Before we can decide that dyslexia is present we first consider the definition.

In 2002, I recommended that we define dyslexia as, '**a difficulty with literacy which results in a person requiring a set of accommodations to be made to enable them to demonstrate their abilities**'.   **Crombie, 2002**.

This means assessing for difficulties with literacy while showing that if accommodations were made (such as being given additional time or the appropriate computer software and hardware) a person could demonstrate their abilities. Until now this definition has not been widely accepted, although examination bodies do consider a student's needs and accept the principle of allowing appropriate accommodations to be made whether or not dyslexia is present. Even though it would seem a short journey to now accept this enabling and inclusive definition without the need for expensive and time-consuming diagnostic assessment, we must all adhere to the definitions adopted by authorities and governments.

In Scotland, the Scottish Government in liaison with Dyslexia Scotland and the Cross-Party Group on Dyslexia in the Scottish Parliament have agreed and established the following definition:

> *Dyslexia can be described as a continuum of difficulties in learning to read, write and/ or spell, which persist despite the provision of appropriate learning opportunities. These difficulties often do not reflect an individual's cognitive abilities and may not be typical of performance in other areas.*
>
> The impact of dyslexia as a barrier to learning varies in degree according to the learning and teaching environment, as there are often associated difficulties such as:
>
> - auditory and/or visual processing of language-based information
> - phonological awareness
> - oral language skills and reading fluency
> - short-term and working memory
> - sequencing and directionality
> - number skills
> - organisational ability.
>
> Motor skills and co-ordination may also be affected.
>
> **Scottish Government, 2018**

They accept that:

> *Dyslexia exists in all cultures and across the range of abilities and socio-economic backgrounds. It is a hereditary, life-long, neurodevelopmental condition. Unidentified, dyslexia is likely to result in low self-esteem, high stress, atypical behaviour, and low achievement.*
>
> *Learners with dyslexia will benefit from early identification, appropriate intervention and targeted effective teaching, enabling them to become successful learners, confident individuals, effective contributors and responsible citizens.*

This definition is now widely accepted throughout Scotland. However throughout the rest of the UK and much of the world, there is no one single definition that covers all authorities, schools and colleges. It is important therefore that teachers know and understand whichever definition is accepted by their establishment.

The definitions adopted by the British Psychological Society (1999) and later by Sir Jim Rose in his 2009 review of dyslexia are perhaps the most widely accepted in England and Wales.

> *'Dyslexia is evident when accurate and fluent word reading and/or spelling develops very incompletely or with very great difficulty. This focuses on literacy learning at the "word" level and implies that the problem is severe and persistent despite appropriate learning opportunities'*
>
> **British Psychological Society 1999**, p.64

> *Dyslexia is a learning difficulty that primarily affects the skills involved in accurate and fluent word reading and spelling.*
>
> *Characteristic features of dyslexia are difficulties in phonological awareness, verbal memory and verbal processing speed.*
>
> *Dyslexia occurs across the range of intellectual abilities.*
>
> *It is best thought of as a continuum, not a distinct category, and there are no clear cut-off points.*
>
> *Co-occurring difficulties may be seen in aspects of language, motor co-ordination, mental calculation, concentration and personal organisation, but these are not, by themselves, markers of dyslexia.*
>
> *A good indication of the severity and persistence of dyslexic difficulties can be gained by examining how the individual responds or has responded to well-founded intervention.*
>
> **Rose, 2009**, p.9 and 29

As we would expect, there are considerable similarities in the definitions. All three emphasise difficulties with reading and spelling and stress that the problems are likely to be severe and persistent, and that this can be shown by considering how an individual responds to well-founded intervention with appropriate learning opportunities. While the accompanying documentation touches on what might be considered as appropriate intervention and learning approaches, they are imprecise in this regard.

It is clear that before we can assume an individual has dyslexia we must consider these factors.

> Assessment of dyslexia is therefore a process considering learning and teaching and the progress made, rather than a single act of assessment.

Confirmation however, may be through standardised assessment preceded by a full diagnostic résumé of previous learning history. It is also important to note that dyslexia is not the only factor to consider. There are often overlaps into other areas such as dyspraxia, dysgraphia, attention deficit disorder (ADD) or attention deficit with hyperactivity disorder (ADHD) or dyscalculia – in fact co-occurrence of dyslexia and other difficulties is common. While consideration of all factors is important, here we consider dyslexia while bearing in mind the importance of other factors and the likelihood of overlap.

Another factor we would wish to consider is whether or not dyslexia is a **specific** learning difficulty or a more **general** difficulty. If it is specific, it will affect the areas described in the definition. If it is more general, it will probably affect all of the individual's functioning skills to some extent. This will make a difference for the child or young person, as it is often the fact that there is a discrepancy between what the learner knows and understands and what they can read and write about that causes the frustrations that can demoralise the individual and destroy their confidence. This also has implications for the teacher as if teachers believe a child is working to their capacity, their perceptions may or may not be accurate and their actions and reactions may not be appropriate.

While we do need to acknowledge that dyslexia is on a continuum and covers all levels of ability, it is the frustrations felt by children and their parents that too often characterise the dyslexia situation. It was for this reason that in 2002 I suggested the previously mentioned working definition of dyslexia:

> *'Dyslexia is a difficulty with literacy which results in a person requiring a set of accommodations to be made to enable them to demonstrate their abilities'.*
>
> **Crombie, 2002**, p.223

For those with dyslexia therefore recognition would not require full diagnostic assessment through a specialist assessor, but could be done by a class teacher or other educator who knew the child well and could propose the appropriate accommodations to ensure the young person could show their capabilities without the need to read and write if these were the main areas of difficulty.

> *'Accommodations are defined as the 'set of enabling arrangements which are put in place to ensure that the dyslexic person can demonstrate their strengths and abilities and show attainment.'*
>
> **Crombie, 2002**, p.222

To summarise, when dealing with children and young people it is important to begin the process of intervention as early as possible and monitor how the child responds. There is no need to label the child at the early stages, but it is important to discuss the possibility of dyslexia and ensure that all that can be done is being done. Delaying appropriate teaching and support is unhelpful and may lead to problems of frustration, self-esteem, behaviour and possible future mental health issues. It is important also to establish just what the child is good at, and ensure these positive factors are taken into account in our teaching.

Having gone through a process of intervention with on-going monitoring, there comes a point where it is important for the child, their parents and teachers to establish the exact nature of difficulties. While it should not be necessary to have a full diagnostic assessment before appropriate teaching and support (in-class and for examinations) takes place, all too often this is the case. Often too parents/carers wish to establish the exact nature of difficulties so arrange for a full diagnostic assessment to be done. At this point it is important for everyone to understand what might be assessed and why.

It is at this point too that specialist skills are required to consider the assessed profile and what it means for life within and outside the classroom and at later stages. We must always remember that those with dyslexia will have areas of strength that can be used to accelerate progress within the difficult areas.

Schools and local authorities will vary in the methods they use to assess for specific learning difficulties and dyslexia following the monitoring process. However given below are some of the current tools available that are standardised in an attempt to ensure parity in establishing those with and without the dyslexia label. Though standardised assessment is not and should not be the criteria leading to appropriate intervention and support, it is currently necessary for those approaching entry to college or university who wish to apply for funding through the Disabled Students' Allowance. It is quite possible that this will change in the future.

It is not necessary for children and young people who require the provision of assessment arrangements for exams to have had a full diagnostic assessment though it does sometimes help clarify the nature of the difficulties and what support is likely to be necessary. It should be noted that anything that is put in place for exams should be the normal practice for that young person and should begin as early as possible in the young person's school career.

FULL DIAGNOSTIC ASSESSMENT

It is important to consider the difference between screening and full diagnostic assessment at this point.

Screening can be for a number of reasons and though it can identify learners that we suspect may be dyslexic or have other difficulties, it is not the same as full diagnostic assessment. Screening can be by the use of a checklist where we register specific areas of concern and what is done to tackle these, or it can be through the use of online tools where similar items to the checklist are presented to learners in a fun and interesting way. Whatever the medium, screening should determine any gaps in the individual's skills and knowledge and lead to specific approaches designed to make up for any gaps found in young people's skills and knowledge. It can also be a pointer to further assessment that is likely to be necessary – for example, to determine if dyslexia should be investigated or if other factors require to be considered.

If the label 'dyslexia' is to help those who have it as well as those who seek to help – their teachers, parents, family, friends and others - then we must be able to provide objective evidence to confirm dyslexia and to provide indications of the most appropriate teaching and support to help. While many may question the efficacy of standardised psychometric assessment, it is the most objective means we have of gaining evidence, and can confirm the suspicions we already have gained through more subjective observational means.

Our starting point for diagnostic assessment must be our definition. Factors noted in the definition MUST be assessed, but in order to establish the best approaches to teaching and learning, it will be important to consider factors that underlie any difficulties found. For example, if we establish that there is a word reading difficulty, we should consider the learner's ability in understanding of phonology and phonics, the basics for word reading, and essential skills for any of us if we meet an unfamiliar word.

Visual memory too is important for memory of irregular words. For young children, the assessment will determine our teaching programme. For older children we can check what has previously been taught in this area, identify the gaps, and put steps in place to address these omissions.

Full diagnostic assessment for those at school will only be necessary if we require to confirm dyslexia, or if assessment is required for purposes of making additional classroom/examination accommodations or for gaining funding (Disabled Students' Allowance, for example, when the student is going on to Higher Education).

However, for purposes of monitoring progress too, some forms of standardised assessment may be desirable. This will allow teachers to gain insight into the speed of progress, and if this is not as hoped, then further measures may be required. These measures should not just tackle the academic areas, but also any self-esteem and motivation issues. See section on Self-esteem and Motivation for more information on how to help. Assessment will also tell us areas where the student is coping adequately and does not need specific targeted intervention. Examples of appropriate material for diagnostic assessment of children displaying a group of indicators are listed below. Please note that no specific editions are mentioned as tests are regularly updated and new versions become available. It is important to use the most recent versions of tests, as these will have more up-to-date standardisations. These can be checked with the test publishers.

Reading

All aspects of reading (Single word reading, decoding, prose reading, rate of reading, comprehension) are important, especially for older children and young people. Any one aspect can affect performance across the board. Slow reading and fluency will affect comprehension. It may also affect a person's ability to finish tasks in a limited time. We would therefore wish to establish exactly why the individual is experiencing difficulties and the areas that are likely to need support for work in class and examinations. These might be, for example, direct teaching, developing study and coping strategies and/or the use of assistive technology.

- Test of Word Reading Efficiency TOWRE: Phonics and word reading, speed and fluency of word and non-word recognition.

- Wechsler Individual Achievement Test (WIAT-T): Prose reading, single word reading, fluency (speed), oral expression, listening and reading comprehension, spelling, maths fluency, maths problem solving (maths in recent edition of test).

- York Assessment of Reading for Comprehension (YARC): Word reading, phonological skills, alphabet knowledge, passage reading for accuracy, fluency and comprehension.

- Wide Range Achievement Test (WRAT): word reading, sentence comprehension – also considers spelling and numeracy.

Spelling

- Wechsler Individual Achievement Test (WIAT)
- Wide Range Achievement Test (WRAT)

Underlying ability (if this is contained in the definition and you are looking for discrepancies and differences as well as strengths)

- Wide Range Intelligence Test (WRIT)
- Reynolds Intellectual Assessment Scales (RIAS)

Handwriting

- Detailed Assessment of Speed of Handwriting (DASH) and DASH17+ for older age groups

Writing

Handwriting, handedness, creative writing, vocabulary use, grammar, syntax, copying, speed of writing in different circumstances. Children with literacy difficulties are often reluctant writers and this in itself should be noted. Discussion with the child and his parents and teacher of why there is reluctance to write may reveal useful information.

Word processing

Presentation, speed, spelling, grammar, syntax, creativity, vocabulary use, touch-typing or not. As word processing can often alleviate difficulties with handwriting, there should be investigation of current skills and the likelihood word processing may reduce handwriting difficulties. This can be assessed by comparing directly with the handwriting tasks. Report in words per minute and consider other factors qualitatively.

Numeracy (essential if included in definition, but also important for planning teaching and support)

- Wide Range Achievement Test (WRAT),
- Wechsler Individual Achievement Test (WIAT-T),

or assess qualitatively according to expectations of the curriculum.

If more detailed information is required on mathematics Feifer Assessment of Mathematics (FAM) gives information on underlying processing which will indicate more precise areas of strength and weakness and will help inform teaching.

Memory (essential if included in definition, but also important for planning teaching and support)

Though only necessary if referred to in the definition, it is also desirable to be aware of the memory skills or lack of memory skills, as this is liable to affect the whole of an individual's functioning.

- Test of Memory and Learning (TOMAL)
- Wide Range Assessment of Memory and Learning (WRAML).

Phonology (important not just if contained in definition but to establish if there is a lack of awareness or knowledge of phonics and ability to use and manipulate sounds.

- Comprehensive Test of Phonological Processing (CTOPP).

Speed of processing information

- Comprehensive Test of Phonological Processing (CTOPP) subtests of speed of naming (digits, letters, objects), speed of reading and writing (words per minute).

Note: these are only a sample of the wide range of material available. We do need to check that the assessment material is suitable for the age of the learners we are testing. In the UK, the best information can be obtained by checking with the Specific Learning Difficulties Assessment Standards Committee (SASC) and Specific Learning Difficulties Test Evaluation Committee (STEC) websites, and using the most up-to-date version of the tests that we can find.

We should of course check the young person's health and fitness on the day we are testing and ensure they are not adversely affected by a temporary illness or health problem. We need also to ensure that hearing and eyesight have been checked. If the young person seems to be sensitive to different lighting arrangements or to different colours of paper, then further investigation may be necessary. (See later sections on Visual Stress and Auditory Discrimination for more information). When conducting an assessment we must also put learners at their ease if we are to establish just what they are capable of and ensure a valid assessment.

Qualitatively, the learner's interests and hobbies will be important, and we need to consider the child or young person's attitudes to the various aspects of the assessment and how motivation varies throughout the assessment dependent on the specific tasks involved.

We should try to use material that is up-to-date and well standardised so validity and reliability are good. Assessment should take account of the culture of the child, and all relevant factors should be noted when reporting the results. Assessment takes place at a particular time on a specific day when for a variety of reasons, the child's performance may not indicate precisely how much they are capable of. To take account of the likelihood that our results will be imprecise, we consider confidence intervals – the limits within which we can feel confident that the learner's true score lies. The 95% interval is generally considered best – we are then 95% confident of our results lying in a particular range. The assessment manuals will help us establish these parameters.

WHAT TO LOOK FOR IN THE RESULTS

Dyslexia

Dyslexia in Scotland is by agreement of the Scottish Government, Dyslexia Scotland and the Cross Party Group on Dyslexia in the Scottish Parliament defined as:

"a continuum of difficulties in learning to read, write and/or spell, which persist despite the provision of appropriate learning opportunities. These difficulties often do not reflect an individual's cognitive abilities and may not be typical of performance in other areas.

The impact of dyslexia as a barrier to learning varies in degree according to the learning and teaching environment, as there are often associated difficulties such as:

- *auditory and /or visual processing of language-based information*
- *phonological awareness*
- *oral language skills and reading fluency*
- *short-term and working memory*
- *sequencing and directionality*
- *number skills*
- *organisational ability.*

Motor skills and co-ordination may also be affected."

Scottish Government, 2018

As has been considered previously, the definition by which we determine if a person has dyslexia or not is critical to how we assess and draw conclusions. We must therefore assess the areas considered by the definition we are using before we can draw a conclusion.

> For a complete diagnostic dyslexia assessment the teacher needs to be satisfied that the whole profile is being considered and that there is a complete picture of strengths and weaknesses.

The test material on the previous pages should be useful but additionally some more precise testing (for example, of phonics, co-ordination or other factors) will be helpful to determine precise strengths and weaknesses so that the areas of difficulty can be tackled.

There is no one pattern for dyslexia, but the following pages set out what to look for and how this can be done. There is much that the class teacher can do with regard to the assessment, but if difficulties are more complex, then help may be required from a specialist either within or outside the school. However unless the child is in an older age group when future career choices are looming, this should be a process starting with the classroom teacher, parent or young person. The classroom teacher's assessment and focused teaching should then determine if detailed assessment with help from specialists will be required and the timescale involved in the process. If there is doubt, then it is best to play safe, and ensure steps are put in place to confirm the initial concerns.

Executive Functioning

Though there can be an overlap between executive functioning difficulties and dyslexia, the two should not be confused. Children with executive functioning difficulties often exhibit some of the signs of dyslexia. They struggle with organisation and planning, they have difficulty managing time. Often there are difficulties with short-term and working memory, sustaining attention over a fairly short period of time, and anticipatory awareness. The young person may struggle to anticipate what will happen if for example, we don't do our essay tonight and we know it will take us at least two hours and we have to hand it in by 3pm tomorrow.

The person with executive functioning difficulties may not anticipate that tomorrow morning there may be other priorities that will have to be dealt with. In this instance they opt to spend the evening watching a film – then realise the next day that there is simply not enough time to complete the work. They didn't anticipate that they would have to go and see their maths tutor about a completely different project. They may also daydream a lot which doesn't help. This type of problem affects most people to some extent but those with executive functioning problems will find this type of occurrence a frequent event and the difficulties encountered will have a significant impact on their everyday life.

The Harvard Center on the Developing Child (2017) define executive function and self regulation as the mental processes that enable us to plan, focus attention, remember instructions, and juggle multiple tasks successfully. According to Cooper-Kahn and Dietzel (2008) executive functions are a set of processes concerning managing oneself and one's resources in order to achieve a goal. It is an umbrella term for the neurologically-based skills involving mental control and self-regulation.

Though there is often an overlap between dyslexia and executive functioning difficulties the two are not the same, and it is quite likely that people will have one without the other. What is important is that the definition of dyslexia is followed. If there are no reading, writing or spelling difficulties and no history of these, then the individual is not dyslexic even though they have memory and organisation difficulties. However this will become clear in the course of the assessment.

If your definition considers dyslexia as a specific learning difficulty then we will need to determine if the difficulties displayed are **specific** or **general**.

The graphs below demonstrates clearly how this can be done. When we assess learners, it helps if we can consider how the scores we get relate to the average. The normal distribution, often represented by a bell curve, is generally familiar to teachers and is useful in describing the frequency of standardised test scores. It can be useful in comparing scores between tests.

If we consider standard age scores, average scores centre around the mean of 100 – thus taking one standard deviation above (115) and one below (85), a score lying between 85 and 115 would be considered 'average'. Scores above 115 would be above average and those below 85 would be 'below average'. The group with scores between 85 and 115 account for 68.26% of the population. If we consider two standard deviations, we cover 95.44% of the population. These learners will have scores lying between 70 and 130.

NORMAL DISTRIBUTION

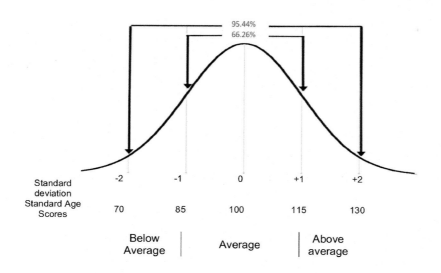

> Standardised tests are designed to follow the normal distribution curve so are a useful means of comparison. Standard scores are generally well understood by the majority of teachers. Reading age scores are also well understood but are best avoided as they do not serve to motivate or encourage children (or their parents), particularly when these are very low.

CASE STUDIES

The following profiles give an indication of what we might look for in determining whether a child has specific learning difficulties or more general learning difficulties.

Josh - General learning difficulties

Josh, age 9, is a good natured boy who comes from a stable two parent family living with his Mum, Dad and two sisters. Neither of his sisters seems to have any particular difficulties though neither of them is outstanding academically. Both of Josh's parents work in a local factory, Dad as a team manager and Mum works on an assembly line as a packer. Josh is generally a healthy child who enjoys watching sport. His school attendance is good with only a few isolated missed days since he started school. Hearing and eyesight are fine though Josh can sometimes seem inattentive.

Josh has a standard score for general underlying ability of 71. His visual and verbal scores are below average and even when confidence intervals are considered. Josh is clearly scoring below average in general ability. He has been drilled in spelling at school, and his parents have supported this at home. Spelling patterns however are not well established and Josh often struggles and is unsure of many common words. Josh knew most of his letters and a few basic word spellings but made many errors in quite basic phonic words. His spelling score was 69, less than his word reading which has also been drilled. Josh enjoys listening to stories but his reading, though better than spelling, is still weak though he is making progress. Numeracy too is very weak. Josh recognises and can identify the numbers to ten and understands the numbers up to five. However adding even just two single numbers is hard for him. Concepts such as time and money are still at a very early stage. He is receiving extra support to try to make headway at a faster pace, but progress continues at a very slow rate frustrating his class teacher and his parents.

Josh comes across as an immature child who seems unaware of other people's irritation at his pace of development. Josh's support teacher feels Josh is doing his best and feels he will get upset if he is pushed further. She feels Josh has general learning difficulties.

A sample of writing reveals that Josh is making reasonable progress and is trying very hard. His handwriting is legible and neatly spaced though still quite immature. He is being taught to join his letters and is coping well. Josh's approach to words shows that he is using the skills he has been taught – he has learned about silent 'e' but has unfortunately applied it wrongly to the word Spain. Josh is starting to come to terms with punctuation and already understands when to start and finish a sentence and when to use capital letters though he still makes occasional errors with punctuation.

Josh - General learning difficulties - Test results

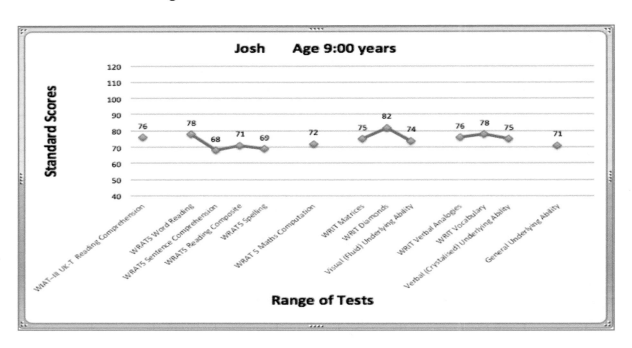

Josh - Handwriting sample

> Josh
>
> My name is Josh. I liv in Glasgo
> with my ~~sma~~ mum and gran.
> I lick holidys. My favrit place is
> spane. Last yer I went to Spane with
> my gran.

Sandi - Specific Learning Difficulties

Sandi (10 years, 2 months) is slightly older than Josh. She also struggles with word reading, spelling and written work. Her understanding of what she reads is limited due to her difficulty in decoding words. When a story is read to her she can answer questions and clearly understands the content. Numeracy though limited by her ability to read the questions accurately, is reasonable though she does need help to demonstrate her knowledge fully. Sandi's general underlying ability however is average to high average and much better than her literacy scores would indicate, especially her writing. She is articulate and has a good understanding of English vocabulary though this does not come across in her writing. Her visual skills too are good and she is able to visualise patterns and reproduce them accurately. She enjoys puzzles and has ability to reason why certain patterns fit and others don't. Sandi's teacher sometimes gets frustrated with her and feels she can be lazy, not paying enough attention to her spelling as she sometimes spells words correctly in one sentence and then gets the wrong spelling in the next.

Sandi - Specific Learning Difficulties - Test results

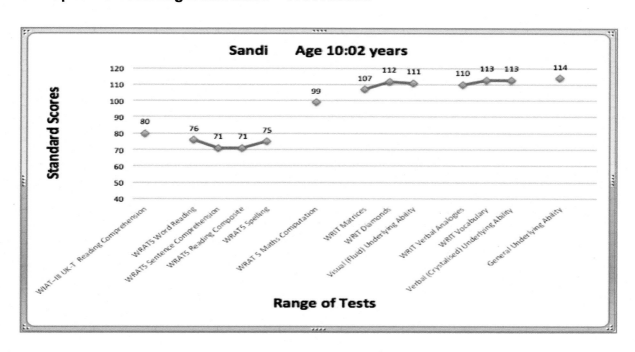

Sandi regularly gets upset as though she tries hard she is unable to work out when a word is wrongly spelled. Her handwriting too makes her teacher think Sandi is lazy. Sandi has mild asthma, but this has not affected her attendance at school which has been generally good. Hearing and eyesight have both been checked recently and both were found to be good. There are no other health concerns. Sandi's parents are extremely anxious about her lack of achievement in reading and written language. Sandi has an older brother and a sister at the same school, neither of whom appear to be having particular problems.

Sandi is an extremely articulate child. She is considered to be reasonably good at maths but has had considerable difficulties in learning multiplication tables and in telling the time. Sandi is far from being the worst in the class and fits the picture of the 'puzzling underachieving' child. A look at the home background reveals Sandi too is from a stable home and lives with her Dad and his partner. Though her Mum and Dad have been separated for a few years, Sandi sees her Mum regularly at weekends. Sandi's Dad had similar difficulties at school but his difficulties were put down to his poor attendance and his lack of attention when in class. He left school at the age of 16 but now successfully manages his own technology business. Sandi's Mum was born in the Caribbean, but spoke English from an early age. She had no particular difficulties at school, and learned English relatively easily.

Sandi - Handwriting sample

My name is Sandi. I have a sister and (a) brother. I am ten years old. I live in Newcastle and my sister is called Jen and my brother is Mac. Mac is on (a) high school trip in London. My brother's good at football and Jen likes tennis.

A closer look at Sandi's writing reveals that Sandi was reluctant to start writing, having three attempts to really get started. Thereafter her writing reveals many and frequent errors - reversals (s and d), problems over when to capitalise letters, lack of punctuation, spelling problems and poor understanding of phonic regularities ('o' 'o' for /oo/, i-e for /ī/ [v-e]), auditory discrimination problems (/f/, /v/ and /th/ - have, brother, live), uncertainty about directionality in forming letter shapes (S in Sandi even though she has written her name innumerable times, s in Newcastle, d in and), difficulty with high frequency and common words, merging letters (si), irregular spacing between letters and words, missing syllables, letters and words.

Sandi has been taught about silent 'e' but is very confused, sometimes adding the 'e' when it is not required and sometimes missing it entirely. Sandi has learned some phonics as can be understood by close reading of her written work ('my' is fine but she has over-generalised the /ī/ sound at the end of a word – 'hy' for 'high'. This however resembles that of a very much younger child and does not reflect her level of ability as illustrated by her oral skills and tasks that do not involve written literacy. **From inspection of Sandi's profile, we have every reason to conclude that Sandi is dyslexic.**

So if we consider the above graphs, we can see that Josh's underlying ability is in the below average category with slightly stronger Verbal ability than Visual. His reading ability and spelling are in line with his other capabilities and his underlying abilities as measured on the WRIT. Confidence intervals at 95% confirm our assumptions that Josh has **general learning difficulties**.

Sandi however has similar reading and spelling abilities, but when considered alongside her underlying Visual and Verbal abilities we can see her difficulties are not across the board (**general**), but are **specific** to areas of literacy. We can therefore say that Sandi has **specific learning difficulties - dyslexia**.

While it is acknowledged that dyslexia can affect all ability levels, it is still possible to observe discrepancies in children with lower ability levels, though these will be smaller and less marked.

If however dyslexia is considered to be a more general difficulty in learning to read, write and spell, then it will not be necessary to establish a discrepancy in performance between underlying ability and attainment in literacy tasks. We must carefully and systematically consider the learner's profile alongside the definition of dyslexia that we use and consider the areas outlined in the definition. When this has been done, it will be clear whether or not the individual meets the criteria set by the definition. Expectations must then be adapted to the profile that is established through assessment.

It is important to observe specific areas of difficulty, as this is often a cause of severe frustration for children and adults with dyslexia. They know they know but can't demonstrate in reading and writing that they know, resulting in loss of self-esteem and morale, and affecting learning - often a downward spiral. We must always bear in mind the limitations of assessing a score of underlying ability. The figures arrived at do not remain fixed throughout life. There is always the possibility that the scores were obtained on an 'off-day'. The scores are nonetheless useful provided they are used in a positive way for the sole purpose of comparing a child's attainment with their likely capabilities. The previous profiles however give examples of what we might look for in recognising dyslexia. Initial investigation of strengths and weaknesses should be carried out in the classroom, but more detailed assessment may require the help of specialist practitioners.
If in doubt, more specialised help should be requested.

For the teacher to suspect dyslexia, we would expect **reading** and **spelling** to be considerably below what we would anticipate for the level of underlying ability and/or oral proficiency. If the learner is required to **hand-write**, then that too would be expected to be clearly below expected levels.

If referring to a test of underlying ability, we would expect a child functioning at average level of around a 100 standard score to have reading, spelling and written ability around the same level. If the ability level were at a higher level, then we would expect reading, spelling and written work to be higher. Though we would not necessarily expect a match, a difference of 15 points or more would be considered worthy of investigation.

In circumstances where the learner has had a significant amount of help and support in school and at home, then a smaller gap may indicate that further investigation is required. Difficulties that persist in spite of on-going targeted teaching should always warrant further attention to ascertain if dyslexia or other specific learning difficulty is present. We must always however bear in mind the limitations of standardised testing. They give a snapshot of a learner's abilities at a certain time on a certain day, and can be influenced by numerous factors such as: level of motivation, tiredness, mood, general health, medication, time of day. Environmental and emotional factors will inevitably affect the learners' ability to concentrate and produce their best responses. It is essential therefore to ensure the learner is put at ease and that there is no unnecessary stress involved at time of assessment.

In the previous examples, we considered Josh to have **general learning difficulties** with his results all falling in the below average category, some well below average. Sandi on the other hand, was considered to have **specific learning difficulties** with only some areas being below what we would expect from considering her underlying ability and level of oral functioning. As Sandi's difficulties lay in the specific areas of word and sentence reading and spelling as well as handwritten work, in the light of the definitions given on previous pages, we conclude Sandi has dyslexia.

While every case will not be as clear cut as these, if there are grounds for suspecting specific learning difficulties, this will require further investigation. If, as a class teacher, you feel unqualified to carry out a dyslexia assessment yourself, it is best to be cautious and refer the child on to whoever in the school has this responsibility. The appropriate channels for further assessment and for obtaining advice on appropriate teaching programmes have already been set out. Be sure to pass on the details of your own assessment and findings, as it may not be necessary to carry out all the tests again. Parents should of course be involved and kept informed of what is happening with their child at all stages in the process, responsibility for arranging contact with parents generally resting primarily with the head teacher in primary schools and likely to be the Support for Learning Co-ordinator in secondary though various factors such as size and nature of school may be important. It should be emphasised that the earlier a child is identified with dyslexia or other specific difficulty the better the prospects. Even in areas and schools where specialist help is available there is generally a time to wait to receive help.

It is therefore essential that class teachers are equipped with the skills to provide support and targeted intervention at all points in the child's journey through school. For teachers who would like to acquire more specialised knowledge, training is available. (**Appendix 3** gives more details.)

For all learners who are experiencing difficulties, even if these are mild, more detailed assessment will be required to establish exactly where the learner is at and where there are gaps in knowledge. We can gain a considerable amount of information from standardised assessment that can guide our teaching; we can for example do some detailed analysis of aspects such as free writing, spelling and numeracy so we can identify exactly where difficulties lie. We then know which areas will require additional teaching and which skills are already competent.

CRITERION-REFERENCED ASSESSMENTS

These are designed to measure a learner's performance against a predetermined set of expectations and criteria. They are regularly used in primary schools to consider how far a child has reached in phonics, reading, number work and similar areas and can identify specific gaps which teachers can then attempt to bridge. They are generally considered preferable to standardised tests that compare children with their peer group.

The value of criterion-referenced assessment should be taken into consideration at all times as it is important for drawing up a plan for further work. In addition to criterion-referenced materials produced by the well-known publishers, schools can also devise their own systems for criterion-referenced assessment based on the curriculum as defined by individual school policy and national guidance. There is a sample of the type of criterion-referenced material available in many schools and local authorities on the following pages.

Phonics Check

Whatever the profile obtained, if the child is experiencing difficulties with phonics, then detailed assessment is required so that an appropriate teaching programme can be put in place. That programme should be multisensory and structured to include the specific teaching of points the child is uncertain of. Assessment tools will probably be non-standardised but will include a breakdown of subskills required for word recognition and reading.

Most schools will have their own version of a phonics checklist beginning with common single letters and moving on to consonant digraphs such as sh, ch and blends such as sp, nt etc. The checklist should work in harmony with the order in which phonics are taught within the school.

Do check that children can not only recognise the letters but can also decode them once they have mastered enough to make up simple cvc words, words with a digraph etc then with a clear progression. They should also be able to recognise the letter when the letter sound is given and should quickly learn to differentiate between letter names and sounds. Letter names are constant so should be used for spelling whereas sounds can vary – for example, the letter 'a' making an /ă/ sound (cat), an /ā/ sound (acorn) or an /ŏ/ sound (was).

Teaching phonics

There are many methods of teaching phonics and each has its critics. While synthetic and analytic phonics have been researched and there are advocates for both, there are many academic arguments about what really constitutes 'reading', and whether decoding is 'reading'. There are other methods of dealing with phonics (such as Phono-Graphix ®) that acknowledge both the analytic and synthetic methods and also have a well-researched base. What is clear is that children need to learn to blend, segment and manipulate phonemes in order to 'crack the code'. When this is done through clear cumulative multisensory structured teaching of phonics, comprehension should result from an ability to recognise and understand words. This is ultimately why we learn to read. A simple phonics checklist will determine just what a child knows and what we need to teach. Teaching of course must ensure that the child has reached the point of automaticity so decoding becomes automatic and comprehension ensues.

			Note any difficulties
1	**Letters/Sounds**		
		Knows all letter sounds a,b,c,d,e,f,g,h,I,j,k,l,m,n,o,p,q,r,s,t,u,v,w,x,y,z A,B,C,D,E,F,G,H,I,J,K,L,M,N,O,P,Q,R,S,T,U,V,W,X,Y,Z	
		Knows letter names a,b,c,d,e,f,g,h,I,j,k,l,m,n,o,p,q,r,s,t,u,v,w,x,y,z A,B,C,D,E,F,G,H,I,J,K,L,M,N,O,P,Q,R,S,T,U,V,W,X,Y,Z	
2	**Letter Matching**	**Can match plastic letters when shown one:** a,b,c,d,e,f,g,h,I,j,k,l,m,n,o,p,q,r,s,t,u,v,w,x,y,z A,B,C,D,E,F,G,H,I,J,K,L,M,N,O,P,Q,R,S,T,U,V,W,X,Y,Z	
3	**Sound – letter Matching**	**Can pick out the letter from a rainbow arc when given a single sound** *(Take lower case and capitals separately):* a,b,c,d,e,f,g,h,I,j,k,l,m,n,o,p,q,r,s,t,u,v,w,x,y,z A,B,C,D,E,F,G,H,I,J,K,L,M,N,O,P,Q,R,S,T,U,V,W,X,Y,Z	
		....	
7	**Sound awareness**	**Recognises initial sound in words – What letter does 'ant', boy, 'cat' etc begin with? Point to the letter. For 'cat', this could be 'c' or 'k' and either would be considered correct here as we are establishing sound awareness. If child points to the 'k', it is best just to say, "Okay" as the sound is correct.** *If there are difficulties here, it will be wise to check auditory discrimination.*	

Happy Valley Primary School   Phonics Check

Happy Valley Primary School - Auditory Discrimination Check

Tell me if these words are the same or different. *(The child should not watch your lips as you say them, so you may need to turn away or put a paper between you and the child so they can't visually determine the answer).*

Use natural speech and say the words with correct pronunciation. **Tick as appropriate**		Discriminating	Same	Different	Notes
1	word - sword	/w/ and /s/			
2	cat - cart	/t/ and /rt/			
3	same - fame	/s/ and /f/			
4	bin - din	/b/ and /d/			
5	line - line				
6	very - merry	/v/ and /m/			
7	fine - vine	/f/ and /v/			
8	merry - Mary	/ĕ/ and /ā/			
9	lamp - lamp				
10	ant - and	/t/ and /d/			
11	last - last				
12	sherry - cherry	/sh/ and /ch/			
13	better - wetter	/b/ and /w/			
14	waiver - waiter	/v/ and /t/			
15	range - range				
16	fair - there	/f/ and /th/			
17	met - meet	/ĕ/ and /ē/			
18	fan - fan				
19	under - wonder	added /w/			
20	Raith - rave	/th/ and /v/			

Before teaching specific phonic points and letters it is best to check that children are able to hear the sounds as they are in words. A test of auditory discrimination should ascertain if the child can hear the sounds we plan on teaching and discriminate between similar sounds. With the help of an auditory discrimination check, you can establish if this is likely to be a problem. If a child can't perceive sounds accurately and know where in words the sounds are heard, it will be almost impossible to spell them correctly.

Training in auditory discrimination is important if the child is found to have some difficulties and hearing has been checked and found to be satisfactory. The child needs to be trained to listen for the sounds in words so they become aware of the relationship between sounds and letters or words and can spell them in the right way. See section on **Training in Auditory Discrimination**.

Memory

From assessment of memory functioning we can generally determine if a learner has short-term and working memory difficulties. Through working memory, information is passed into long-term memory, and this is a process, which very often is ineffective in those with specific literacy difficulties. Aspects of TOMAL and other diagnostic material (generally the Digit and Letter Span tests) can indicate short-term difficulties and the Reverse Span tests will indicate working memory capacity. However, though it is important to know this, it doesn't tell us how much information is liable to be lost prior to it being received into long-term memory – a likely concern for those with dyslexia and other specific learning difficulties. This we can only guess from the information we have. Working memory however is an important holding area for information. Every activity involves the use of working memory.

> If that system is not robust there is likely to be a problem. If pupils go off-task in the classroom or go off at a tangent, then the likelihood is that working memory is problematic. To successfully learn, we require working memory capacity to operate effectively.

Working memory is used when we hold things in memory for short periods of time in order to do something with them – for example, mental arithmetic, recalling directions, following a sequence of instructions. When we deal with words, we are dealing with representations in different parts of the brain: we deal with meaning in one part and physical representation in another. Working memory helps us bring those representations together. If the connections within the brain are not working effectively this inevitably affects the brain's ability to output information accurately. Bringing together the physical shapes of letters with the sounds they make (especially when any slight wavering can turn a 'b' into a 'p', 'q' or 'd') involves working memory so the impact of inefficient working memory is likely to result in very little accurate information becoming set in long-term memory. How we deal with the physical and sensory (speech, hearing, visual, feel of letters and whole words when written or typed) aspects will affect the likely outcomes. The more we use the brain's capacity to integrate sensory experience, the better we support working memory. What we see, hear, say and touch together with what we feel, involve us in building capacity for information to pass through working memory and into long-term memory.

To strengthen auditory channels, we use visual representations such as diagrams, mind maps, the use of colour and highlighting so children not only hear but also see what we want them to remember. We strengthen this by providing stories, listening tasks, getting children to say out and recite. This is made more effective through integration with the kinaesthetic skills of touch-typing, handwriting, acting out and movement. All of these when coordinated and brought together in multi-sensory experiences serve to facilitate the movement of information from working memory to long-term memory for more permanent storage.

Chapter 4

Recording a Learner's Needs and Monitoring Progress

Whether or not dyslexia is the only difficulty that is affecting the young person, it is important to ensure that a record is kept of all screening and assessment information and how it is being used to inform intervention and teaching. Monitoring should be in place to ensure everything that can be done is being done to ensure maximum progress and that this is evaluated over time. Though the legislation varies throughout the UK, teachers are expected to deliver a 'graduated approach' that is reviewed termly and uses an appropriate and effective system of teaching and monitoring. It is unlikely that a child or young person with dyslexia in Scotland will require a Co-ordinated Support Plan (CSP) as these are for young people with wider needs who require services to be co-ordinated between school and another agency (or between agencies) such as Health or Social Work.

In England, however, those with severe dyslexia may require an Education, Health and Care (EHC) Plan. Assessment will determine the severity of needs. Those for whom dyslexia is mild to moderate would be expected to cope through the school's own support mechanisms. Record keeping is important and information must be kept updated so it can be accessed in the event of a teacher being absent. It is also important to maintain records so the pupil's improvement can be readily monitored to feed back to parents regarding year on year progress and show positive feedback whenever possible to the child or young person.

Whatever is established as a result of assessment, children's needs must be addressed and teachers have the main responsibility for ensuring that this happens. Each school will have a pupil support coordinator or SENCo who has responsibility for ensuring the requirements of pupils with additional support needs are met within the school.

Individualised Educational Programmes/Individual Education Plans (IEPs)

An IEP is an individualised document that sets out planned actions to accommodate the needs of a learner that are different from or additional to those in place for others in the same learning context. It is intended to be helpful for all who are involved with the young person and must take account of the strengths of learners as well as individual needs. IEPs are unlikely to be necessary in the early years or early stages of the process leading to assessment. However if severe difficulties are established which cannot be readily met within the classroom and group context, or if there is likely to be significant involvement of another agency, then an IEP may be required.

> IEPs identify the priorities for the child or young person that are not able to be met by the usual classroom differentiation, and what particular steps and resources are going to be required to enable needs to be met.

Needs may still be met within the classroom but with appropriate individualisation and perhaps assistive technology. IEPs should be positive documents that set provision in an inclusive context and give clear plans to help teachers, parents and others collaborate to offer the optimum outcomes for the young person. The young person should wherever possible be involved in determining the content of the plan.

Individual local authorities and schools will have their own proformas for laying out the IEP. This will be linked to their staged assessment and intervention systems. In all there will be space to include long term and short term targets which should be SMART – Specific, Measurable, Achievable, Relevant and should set out a Timescale. Long-term targets are likely to cover a school year with short-term targets being considered achievable within six to eight weeks or a term. Targets should not only be academic, but where appropriate will consider behaviour, attendance and any other factors which are considered relevant to the young person's future outcomes.

At the initial IEP meeting the personnel to be involved in implementation must be identified and their role made clear. Class and subject teachers will play the major role in providing the appropriate support, but other agencies, parents and support staff will work collaboratively with the student to maximise the success of the plan. IEPs require to be regularly monitored and it is often best to set dates for meetings well in advance so that progress towards existing targets can be considered and new targets identified.

There is no hard and fast rule about who should have an IEP. In some schools an IEP may be considered necessary in order to individualise support appropriately. In another where there are many children with similar needs, one may not be required. When individualisation of curriculum or resources is no longer required and the young person is coping without significant change being made, the IEP can be stepped down. This should be agreed at a review meeting and monitoring should be continued to ensure progress is maintained.

No matter the stage the young person has reached in their education, high priority should be given to the early identification of pupils with additional support needs as the earlier needs are identified and met, the better the outcomes are likely to be. The learner who knows and understands their difficulties can be better prepared both emotionally and educationally for the challenges that they will meet.

A robust system of monitoring and tracking should be in place for all those who require additional support. Suggestions are given in the appendices as to how this can be done, but if the local authority or school has a system in place then this should be followed, as consistency and continuity are important considerations. Whether or not there are other plans in place a close record should be kept of any literacy difficulties identified, assessments done (whether these are standardised or criterion referenced), approaches used, specific resources put in place and progress made. Detailed records should be kept of the programme of teaching though these need not be lengthy. When a regular programme of support is in place it helps if record keeping follows a proforma as then the teacher or assistant can keep a regular plan and note progress on this. If lessons are typed up beforehand they can then be annotated while teaching to guide the next teaching session.

All staff need to be aware of the Data Protection Act and ensure that they are compliant, keeping records secure but still available for those who require access. It must be ensured that records are disposed of securely when they are no longer required. It helps if the school has clear policies in place and procedures on information governance are monitored closely.

Chapter 5

Tackling Literacy Difficulties

WHAT CAN BE DONE TO ALLEVIATE PROBLEMS?

Pre-school/Nursery

At this stage the best approach to adopt is the use of games. Activities will all have a purpose designed to improve a number of skills, in particular those that are important for reading and writing. Nonetheless, the child should see all these activities as fun. While we may suspect that a child is likely to have dyslexia and will face difficulties in more formal learning there is no need or desire to label children at this early stage. If we make the activities of a group nature, then all the youngsters in the group are likely to benefit. The suggestions of possible activities and strategies for children that follow can be used before they attend formal schooling. They are designed to improve various important skills at an early stage. There are more activities for the early years suggested in the section on Early Intervention. The possibilities for games are limitless, restricted only by the time and opportunities available.

The use of rhyme, rhythm and alliteration has proved vital in the development of later reading and writing. Research by Torgesen and others has shown that intervention before a child goes to school can and does affect future development. These skills should be encouraged through games, activities, songs and stories that emphasise rhyme and rhythm.

For example:

- Snap games where children identify rhyming pairs of picture cards
- Games where children pick out the one which does not match from a series of rhyming picture cards
- Encourage children to make up silly alliterative sentences:

  Silly Samantha Snake Slithered Slowly............

  Potty Pete Peered Past Polly.........

All children will need considerable help with this at first. Try putting in a word which is out of place and see if children can identify what it is.

  Rich Rude Robert Really Runs Round Rabbits' Houses.

Ask children to identify the first sound they hear in words. It will help if the teacher stresses the first sound till the children get the idea. Once they can do this, the children can then suggest words.

  Lucky Linda Likes Lollies.   What else does she like?

Everything else must start with an /l/ sound – lions, lights, lorries, laughing..

For some children it will be apparent that they have difficulty in any rhyming-type or alliterative activities, and these children will need patient help in a very small group or individually for a time.

- Prompt the child to verbalise sequences of organised motor activities.
- Use music and movement activities to give experience of sequencing, encouraging children to stand in sequence in counting games etc.
- Allow time to organise activities. Talk through what must be done in a sequence and encourage repetition of order before carrying out tasks.
- Ensure a focus of attention before giving instructions or telling a story.
- Encourage listening skills in various ways. For example:

Listening Games

- With eyes closed, identify certain familiar sounds – jingling keys, rustling paper, bang of a drum, clapping hands etc. Children then verbalise.
- Commercially produced recordings of sounds such as aeroplanes, trains etc.
- Commercially produced resources such as 'Talking tins' which record and playback speech, music and sounds.
- Present a short sequence of sounds with children's eyes closed, then omit one sound, and children must spot what has been missed – e.g. clapping, snapping fingers, banging, then omit snapping fingers. Gradually increase the length of the sequence.
- With children seated in a circle, one child is chosen and sits in the middle with eyes closed. Teacher points to another child who must whisper the name of the child in the centre. Child then opens eyes and says the name of whoever whispered his or her name.

- Take every opportunity to praise the child for achievements. Self-esteem is vital to learning at all ages. Encourage the child to further develop any skills in which they seem to achieve success.
- Encourage skills that children will require later, such as the ability to divide words into parts or syllables. Teacher claps the children's names one at a time and children copy. Later individual children try to clap names of other things – animals, toys etc.
- Develop observation, sequencing and memory skills by inviting children to copy a sequence of actions, firstly observing the teacher – hands in the air, walk round chair, stamp feet, nod head etc. Teacher picks a child to copy the sequence.
- Co-ordination skills can be developed by various activities for both gross and fine motor development – bead threading, sequencing beads to match a colour sequence, catching a soft ball, throwing a ball to try to get it into a bucket, picking up a sequence of small cards for matching activities.

The teacher must be aware of children who do not manage well in particular activities, and immediately follow up that activity with one where the child will meet with immediate success.

In School

While appropriate help at an early stage will minimise difficulties later, there will be children who will still require considerable support at a later stage. There will be learners too whose early experiences before coming to school will leave them at a disadvantage when faced with learning to read and write, and these children will need considerable work on vocabulary development, pre-reading and pre-writing skills before being introduced to books and formal letter formation. Many of these children will not be dyslexic, but in the early years, it is often difficult to be sure.

If children's difficulties are relatively mild, or if they are considered to be working to their capacity, then they are unlikely to get any form of external specialist support. Nonetheless, a well-structured programme is essential if these children's problems are to be minimised. The school's SENCo or educational psychologist should be able to give advice in devising a suitable programme for individual children. If a support for learning teacher is available in the school, then valuable help should be available for carrying out the programme.

Children who have specific learning difficulties, even though they may be mild, will require the programme to be of a multisensory nature and structured phonically in such a way that any points which a child is unsure of will be covered methodically and thoroughly in a cumulative way. Diagnostic assessment will determine what must be included in the child's programme.

The class teacher can do a considerable amount to alleviate problems in the classroom. Much can be achieved by adopting a positive outlook towards the child and praising whenever possible. Praise does need to be deserved and well considered as children with dyslexia are generally only too well aware of their own inadequacies and will quickly work out when there is any lack of sincerity if the praise is unwarranted. They do however need constant encouragement to build confidence. The following suggestions might help:

- Give credit for oral responses whenever this is feasible.

- Find alternatives to written responses – art, drama, technology, presentation, photography etc. This should work for the whole class.

- Mark written work for content. While it must be clear that there are spelling errors, do not dwell on this aspect, or the child will become inhibited and unwilling to produce written work. Find other ways of tackling spelling difficulties. Games and computer work as well as a structured multisensory spelling programme that relates to the phonics teaching will be more effective than the child being faced with a plethora of errors. **See Appendix 2 for suggestions on materials.**

- If you give set homework, find out how long it takes the child to complete it at home, and adjust the amount accordingly so that it can be completed in a reasonable time according to the child's age. Children with dyslexia may take hours to complete work that others would do in ten minutes. Homework should be for reinforcement of teaching, and not an ordeal for parents.

- If a child has difficulty in visually tracking along a line, allow the use of a line guide.

- If expecting a child to copy homework, then always check the homework is written down accurately before allowing the work to be taken home.

- In the classroom, seat the child where you can give help easily, but without embarrassing them. Make sure the learner is facing the board or screen, as they may become easily disorientated by having to turn around.

- Get the young person with dyslexia to verbalise numeric and mathematical processes when there is time to consider fully their understanding (or not) of what is involved. This may also help others in the class. In this way any misunderstandings can be explained and other youngsters can help, for example by saying in a small group situation, "Can you think of a way of explaining this that will help Jack to understand?" This makes others too think about the problem and what they are actually doing to get the answer. Ensure that different children receive help at times so no single child is targeted.

- Allow the child to make use of digital equipment to record whenever this is feasible. This will give the child confidence in using the technology and can be used to record answers orally if written work is liable to be illegible or difficult to understand. Learners can also gain enjoyment and increase comprehension and listening skills by listening to recorded books downloaded to tablet or computer. A quiet corner of the classroom will be necessary for this type of work. A range of digital resources is available for this end and the child should be introduced gradually to a full range.   **See Appendix 2, Assistive Technology**.

- Allow the child extra time to copy work from the board or book. With older learners, it may be best to provide a neat copy, photocopy or digital version. This is important particularly if time is limited or the work is liable to be indecipherable.

- Allow the learner extra 'think' time for answering questions. Some young people with dyslexia are slow to process information and need time to think about the question, formulate their answer and be ready to respond with a reasonable degree of confidence.

- If a child is unhappy about reading aloud in class, don't ask them to. Allow the child to join an appropriate group for discussion when this can be managed. Even though written work or reading may not be up to the standard of the higher group, the child with dyslexia will be motivated by being included in discussions which are more suitable for her ability level.

- Give a visual representation of letters that are often flipped or reversed. Allow the child to illustrate this with a mnemonic that will help.

- Teach keyboard skills and touch-typing and encourage practice. See separate section on **Information Technology and Appendix 2**.

- Encourage learners to use their own personal dictionary or wordbook as soon as they are able. Into these they can put words that they find difficult to spell, and words that they may need for various different subject areas.

- Give practice with alphabet sequencing and dictionary skills. Even though digital technology has rendered this skill less essential than it once was, throughout life it will help if there is knowledge of alphabetical order as much information is often sorted by this method. As soon as the child knows the sequence of the letters in the alphabet, they should practise their skills in using a dictionary. This can be tackled as a group activity as there is generally a number of children who will benefit from this practice.

- Teach the children to divide the dictionary into quartiles.

The four quartiles are found by dividing each half of the dictionary. The learner should discover that by halving the dictionary it will open around the letter M. By further halving it, he will then arrive around D in the first half, or S in the second half. Games are often helpful to give reinforcement.

- While individual help for a sustained period of time is not always possible in the classroom situation, try to give a few minutes regularly throughout the day to ensure the child is succeeding at least in some of the work. Where it is not possible to give as much attention as the child needs, consider using the same structured multisensory programme for children with other types of learning difficulties and form a group for this type of teaching. In this situation, groupings have to be flexible as the child will probably be better in a different group for areas of the curriculum not affected by her specific difficulties.

- Allow the child to make use of the computer or a tablet as often as possible. This will help familiarise the learner with the keyboard and build up confidence. Use the computer for reinforcement work, for a fun way of presenting material and for word processing as well as a multitude of other purposes.

- Organisational skills are often weak, and it will help if teachers can suggest ways of helping. Primary teachers, for example, can get the whole class to make a note in their homework diaries that the next day is a gym day and that they must bring their kit. This way, parents will probably see it and make sure that they remember to put their kit in their bags. Having everything labelled with the child's name, class and home address may seem an obvious precaution, but for the child who is liable to mislay things, it is a basic essential.

For older children, they must have multiple copies of their timetable, so that if one gets lost or mislaid, they always have a spare copy. They must keep a copy in a sensible place, such as a Homework notebook where it can readily be consulted. They must know where to find a spare copy if the first gets lost. If using a digital diary, ensure a paper backup is kept in case of accidentally deleting the file.

Parents can help here too by having a large copy of the child's timetable mounted on the child's bedroom wall where it can be consulted each night so that the child always puts the necessary books and kit in her bag for the next day.

- Ensure that text is easy to access. Simple adaptations to factors such as text size and font can make a difference to readability and therefore to understanding of text. Ensure that if you are making your own worksheets or can adapt existing ones, that you consider factors to increase readability.

- Consider typeface and font. The font is the tool that produces the typeface. Some typefaces are easier to read than others so check if the student finds some fonts work better than others. Sans-serif fonts such as Arial (as used in this book) and Century Gothic are generally preferable to serif fonts such as Times New Roman. Check if your students have particular preferences and try to be accommodating while acknowledging that if you have several learners with dyslexia, you may not be able to produce different worksheets to please all.

- Make extra allowances. Your learner may be very tired due to the concentration and effort that they have to make just to keep up.

- Take every opportunity to praise for effort. Even though your learner may not have achieved the standard of his peer group, the pupil with dyslexia may have made considerably more effort than others at the same stage.

- Allow the young person to have a 'study buddy' if this helps. The buddy must be empathetic towards dyslexia and be comfortable to help out with reading or other tasks with which the young person with dyslexia is struggling.

- Try to take learning style into consideration. Teachers may assume that children learn the way they did, which will certainly not always be true. Though some recent research on learning styles has proved equivocal, there is little doubt that many teachers are systematic, sequential learners and adopt this style quite naturally. Many young people with dyslexia however will adopt a holistic, more global approach.

  Awareness that there might be a mismatch between pupil and teacher will lead to increased understanding of why certain pupils find classroom learning difficult. There is much that teachers can do to meet the learning style of individual pupils. **See later section on Learning Styles.**

- Start training the child on memory skills if this is an area of weakness. **See later section on Memory**.

At the secondary stage

Many of the approaches recommended for the primary school are also appropriate at secondary. The transition from primary to secondary school is particularly important as the child has new challenges to face. However, the same learning principles apply at the secondary stage of education as at the primary. However, other issues start to present themselves when the child reaches the secondary school. One of these is the realisation of having several teachers who all have to be made aware the child has specific learning difficulties and how this is likely to affect their particular subject area.

Often the secondary school support for learning teacher will take charge of the process of transition and ensure information from the primary school is available and children can gradually become familiarised with the secondary school in the year before they move over. Secondary teachers can get to know children who may struggle to orientate their way around the school and struggle with aspects of different subjects.

Another challenge for the child with dyslexia is that by the secondary stage time for the process of catching up is running out as important exams start to loom closer. One means of helping poor readers is to consider the possibility of setting up a paired reading scheme within the school. Fifth and sixth year students are facilitated to work with younger children, sometimes using part of their lunch break to help. This of course requires a member of staff to organise and monitor, but the amount of supervision required once the scheme is established is minimal. The benefits to the children are considerable and besides the obvious advantages, there is prestige for first and second year youngsters of having a buddy in the upper school. For the senior pupils this valuable experience can be cited in their CVs and personal statements when applying for university or work.

It becomes increasingly necessary to investigate strategies for sidestepping problems rather than expecting each subject teacher to tackle specific programmes within their own area. A number of circumvention strategies however will probably be required to help the child cope in all the requisite areas of the curriculum (see overleaf).

Some points to consider are:

1. Would the child benefit from having a photocopied or digitised version of the teacher's notes? This is particularly important for the child with handwriting difficulties and/or typing difficulties. Subject teachers should be able to organise this.

2. If it is school policy to have teachers' notes on the school website for students to download, this is likely to help enormously. This will not only help the students with dyslexia but all can benefit from this. Students can then download the study notes to their iPods, tablets or phones. If they playback with earphones no one even knows what they are listening to.

3. Encourage the young person to make their own list of vocabulary that he needs to spell for his different subjects along with the meanings of the different words if required. A pocketsize notebook clearly labelled with name and class is probably best for this. Learners can then list the words either by subject or alphabetically.

4. Provide a template to help students respond to different genres when making notes. This can be in digital as well as written format.

5. A recording device is useful for presenting novels and other material that require significant amounts of reading. A recording of a book can offer the learner a non-judgemental way of practising reading while gaining an understanding of the novel or other material.

    Local authority libraries often have a range of audio books available to download or on disk. Subscription services may be worthwhile for the wide selection of material they offer. However, although the Calibre audio library charges a small fee to join it has a huge range of material that can be accessed by people with dyslexia and other difficulties in reading print. It will be worth considering these.

    For those in Scotland, Call Scotland (http://www.callscotland.org.uk) has a large bank of resources including an open-access Resource Library of specialist books, journals, video and multimedia materials.

6. Would the use of a word processor and/or text-to-speech software benefit the young person? Slow or difficult to read handwriting can be circumvented by the use of technology. Word processing with text-to-speech of the learner's own text is a multisensory feedback loop – thinking, writing, seeing what has been written and then hearing what has actually been written. There is some evidence that the visual image of the words on the screen matching the printed image seen when reading the word in a book helps the child to recognise when a word is not correct. The ability to check spelling that a word processor offers can prove a huge benefit if the learner is able to recognise the words. More importantly the spell checking facility lets the young person know which words to leave alone. Those with dyslexia can be liable to changing correct words that they think look wrong.

When seeking information on the Internet, text-to-speech software can facilitate the reading involved in finding appropriate information. The writer's message then gets from the paper/ print/media to the reader's mind without the necessity for decoding – often a drudge for the learner with dyslexia. This is useful for subject specific and curriculum focused purposes and for enabling students to experience a variety of genres and writers' styles. It is also likely to ensure accuracy of understanding when instructions or knowledge delivery is important for the learner.

7. Predictive text too is helpful, particularly for technical subject-specific vocabulary that the young person is getting to know. It will be necessary to ensure the words are put into the program's dictionary if they are not already there.

8. For children and young people who will benefit from using a laptop for exams and other preparatory work in class, learning keyboard skills is likely to be of great benefit, allowing the young person to attend to the computer screen instead of switching between screen and keyboard which can be very difficult and disorientating for many. The younger the learner starts this the better.

9. Digital scanning pens are a useful aid for reading any words that a student finds difficult. In certain circumstances they can also be used in examinations to ensure the learner is enabled to understand questions without the help of a human reader. Earphones are used to enable the student to stay in the main examination room.

10. Speech-to-text software is an option for young people with literacy difficulties but is liable to be more disruptive in the classroom situation.

11. Arrangements for exams will need to be considered. If technology is granted for the exam situation over and above what is available to other students, then it may be that separate accommodation will be required. Ensure any arrangements you are applying for are already in place and that examination arrangements are applied for in good time. Whatever arrangements are to be made for examinations, these should be the young person's regular way of working and skills should have been practised over a period of time so the student is comfortable with the additional arrangements.

12. Study skills should be taught to all children and generally are, but do consider any additional techniques or strategies which the young person with dyslexia will require as most require to practise much more than others.

Chapter 6

Structured Cumulative Multisensory Approaches

The primary sensory systems concerned with language perception and development are the auditory (hearing), oral (speaking), visual (seeing) and tactile-kinaesthetic (feeling, movement). A problem in these sensory systems may cause specific language difficulties, with subsequent problems in learning and blending sounds and in the sequencing of phonic units and words. Visual, auditory and phonological difficulties can ensue. Thus for reading, neither a 'look and say' nor a 'phonic' approach will succeed on its own or even in combination.

However, success can be achieved when there is co-ordinated interaction of all the requisite senses – when the child sees, hears, writes and speaks simultaneously. This multisensory learning then integrates the visual, auditory, kinaesthetic and oral capabilities of the learner and encourages the use of the child's strengths while at the same time exercising the weak areas. This helps enhance memory and promotes learning.

In learning phonics for example, when a child is learning the letter 'd', he will listen to the teacher say the letter name and the sound /d/. He will look at it, say the letter name and the sound, and he will practise writing the letter on various surfaces - e.g. table, sand tray, piece of velvet, carpet or any other surface which the learner likes and seems to benefit from. He may type too when using a computer or tablet to aid the learning process.

Once the child is ready, a very similar procedure is used in learning to spell words. It is necessary to build the child's knowledge one small step at a time. For this reason the teacher has to be quite sure what the child really knows, and structure the teaching in such a way that the child will build knowledge in a cumulative way, firmly basing new knowledge on that which had been acquired. The teaching then progresses in a clearly devised order. It is of course necessary to record progress methodically so that it is plain for all concerned.

Multisensory learning is about using all the channels of learning to ensure the learner capitalises on the available learning capacity. With children and adults with dyslexia there is usually weakness in one of the sensory channels - auditory (hearing), visual (seeing), oral, (speaking), kinaesthetic (movement, feel). Auditory and visual weaknesses are not so much about what the learner is able to see or hear, though this should always be checked, but about HOW they see and hear - how do they perceive the sounds, see the symbols. Is the brain playing a trick on them? It's not about IF the child can hear the sound /s/ for example in the word 'list' but about where they perceive each letter to be in the word. If the child thinks they hear it as the last sound in the word, they will be very likely to spell it wrongly.

Similarly if the child perceives the letter 'b' wrongly in the word 'band', this could be a visual or an auditory difficulty and could result in the reversal of both the 'b' and the 'd' signifying an auditory difficulty in perceiving sound rather than a purely visual confusion. The brain might hear the sound, but perceive it wrongly as making a /d/ sound, or maybe a /p/ sound, or it may visually be perceived as the other way round or the other way up. Ensuring the child is able to make new connections in the brain by using his senses to reinforce learning will lead to increased ability to decipher letters and words and blend these in the ways needed to become literate. It is the integration of all the incoming information that confuses the dyslexic brain. Simultaneously processing this information (seeing, hearing, saying, writing) through the senses leads to automaticity over time and increased understanding of how the separate systems can be brought together to produce meaningful information.

Auditory discrimination

Auditory discrimination is a processing skill that some children just seem to pick up and others do not. Auditory discrimination, when applied to literacy, is the skill of differentiating between similar sounding letters, so if a child hears a /v/ sound in a word such as 'van', the child knows the word is different from the word 'fan'. The child would also be aware that the sound is at the beginning of the word and not at the end. For children with dyslexia and/or literacy difficulties this skill doesn't always develop automatically.

> Auditory discrimination is about the perception of sounds rather than the hearing of sounds, so even when hearing is perfect there can still be a concern.

Where there are difficulties, it does not mean there is a hearing difficulty as some believe, but it is a strong indication that hearing should be fully checked by an audiometrician. If hearing is checked and is fine, then it can be assumed it is a perception difficulty and the problems lie at recognition and processing level. Auditory discrimination is an essential skill for building up and breaking down words into their constituent sounds. Without ability to recognise sounds and where these sounds are heard in words, children have difficulty in spelling and breaking words down into their individual letter sounds or parts. However the good news is that it can generally be improved through appropriate teaching and support.

For children who are learning to become literate, auditory discrimination involves the recognition of the sounds and syllables that make up words and where in the words these sounds and syllables are found. For teachers, it is important to recognise those children and young people who are struggling, and ensure steps are taken to maximise their potential to interpret the sounds that make up words. This is not so much about being able to hear the sounds. It's about being able to perceive the sounds and where they are heard. If a child is unable to do this, they are likely to have difficulties in spelling. While spelling is not the 'be-all and end-all', it is an important skill for literacy development.

If auditory discrimination has been checked and found to be weak, the first priority would be to check hearing if this has not been done already. A full audiometric check will establish if there is a problem that could result in a child having difficulties with phonics and learning sounds and correspondences.

When teaching phonics and introducing a new sound it is important to always check that the child can hear the sound and is able to recognise where the sound is in a word. For example, when teaching the sound /sh/:

Where in the word 'hush' do you hear the /sh/?
Where do you hear the /sh/ in the word 'shirt'?
Where is it in 'ashen'?
Where in 'abolish'?
Where in 'shrink'?
Where in 'rashly' and so on,

so you ensure the child is aware of the sound and aware also of where they hear it in words.
If they are not then the spelling of the word is likely to suffer accordingly.

Recognising if there is a difficulty

Recognising when there are auditory discrimination difficulties is key to resolving the child's difficulties in this area. Auditory discrimination skills help children make sense of spelling and word attack, and help them resolve why words are built up and broken down in specific ways. There are several ways in which teachers can check children's processing skills and perception of sounds. Tests of phonological awareness might give indications, but there are some specific tests designed to investigate auditory discrimination skills. Some of these tests are freely available and a sample of an auditory discrimination check is given previously in this book.

> Auditory discrimination checks generally present the child with similar sounding words, such as 'there' and 'fair', and the child has to say whether these are the same or different. They sound similar but are completely different words. We need a whole group of similar sounding words that will check all the different sounds to establish if there are some sounds or groups of sounds that are problematic.

Are there specific parts of words that a child finds difficult – perhaps they focus on the start of the word, and the rest gets lost, so they hear sounds if these are at the beginning of a word but wouldn't recognise the sound if it is at the end or even in the middle.

We can ask the child where in a word they hear a specific sound, so "Where do you hear the /s/ in 'hiss', where do you hear it in 'Isobel', where is it in 'lass', where in 'smile'?" and so on till you feel you have established a good picture of strengths and weaknesses. If there are difficulties then this means we need to spend some focused time working on this skill, encouraging the child to hear the sounds.

This means lots of multisensory training work. For example, "We hear a /m/ sound at the start of 'muppet', do you hear the /m/ sound? (Emphasising the sound and ensure you don't say /mĭ/). "What sound comes at the start of 'Milly'? Yes, that's right – it's a /m/". Do this for all the sounds the child finds difficult. For older children or those who are not receiving a programme of teaching, you may decide to only work in the areas of difficulty.

> Whatever the age of the child, learning is more likely to succeed if you work on the particular sound areas of weakness and relate those in a multisensory way to the teaching of the sounds along with the accompanying letters.

Teaching auditory discrimination skills as part of a structured programme of literacy teaching

For example, when teaching the sound /sh/, start by ensuring your child knows if and where they hear the sound, so,

"Do you hear a /sh/ in the word 'hush'?
If they do, "Where in the word do you hear that sound?".
Child should say, 'Beginning', 'Middle' or 'End'.
If they don't hear it or get the positioning wrong,
"Listen again – 'hush' (emphasising the /sh/ sound till you feel sure they can hear it and are aware they are hearing it.
"Let's try another – 'ship'.

Now this time we're also going to make the word 'ship' and make it up with the child so they also see it is at the beginning and really understand what they are doing. Help as much as is required at this stage. When teaching a new sound, check before you start that the child can auditorily discriminate that particular sound. If not, work on it, listening for the sound, ensuring the child can hear it and position it correctly in the word, make it with plastic or wooden letters, say it, write it, say it again, say the sounds as they write, say the word. With practice skills will improve.

Once it has been established that the young person can perceive sounds in their correct position in a word, the effectiveness of the multisensory approach will give maximum benefit. Using a multisensory approach to teaching and learning helps learners get around any minor difficulties in any one sensory area and make the most of their potential for learning - hearing, seeing, saying, doing (writing, acting, singing, physically making the shapes that make the sounds, and any other means of exploiting as many channels of learning as possible simultaneously) gives the learner a better prospect for learning.

> As with all learning, the learner must feel motivated to learn, so irrespective of the age of the learner, novel and innovative ways of teaching and achieving a multisensory approach have to be considered.

A possible structure for planning and recording progress can be established from a variety of sources. There are a number of commercially produced multisensory programmes. **See Appendix 2 for suggestions of structured material** that may be of help.

Cumulative multisensory structured approaches involve both synthetic and analytic teaching and learning. Analytic phonic teaching presents words as a complete unit and encourages learners to work out what the words say from looking at the constituent parts. Analytic phonics are generally used along with a look and say approach, so the learner sees the whole word, and if they don't recognise it they break it into parts. To start children are taught a letter and introduced to lots of words beginning with that letter.

Synthetic phonics teaching on the other hand, presents the parts (phonemes) first and teaches how these phonemes blend together to form words. The letters and the sounds they make are therefore taught and children learn how to put these letters together to sound out words. In reality, though synthetic phonics is advocated by government, children learn how to put together and break up words for the purposes of both reading and spelling. Neither process however can be considered as teaching 'reading'. Reading is about extracting meaning from words and that requires more than phonics. Decoding is certainly a step towards 'reading', and a very necessary one.

Morphology too is important in helping build vocabulary and meaning. Learners study how morphemes are combined to form meaning and words. This is considered more fully in the reading section that follows.

Placing a learner on a cumulative structured multisensory programme will require some in-depth assessment. If using an established programme, assessment material is likely to be supplied as part of the programme so a teacher can establish where to place the child. Once the learner's phonic knowledge is established and any gaps identified, a plan is made on how to best progress learning. Considerable care must be taken to ensure learners are not pushed at too fast a pace, as this is likely to undo any good that is gained.

A steady pace with lots of reinforcement and fun activities for ensuring overlearning will generally produce the desired results. No one pace will suit all so careful consideration must be given, and lessons tailored to the individual needs of the learner. Only when a teacher has gained experience of a number of programmes will the teacher feel competent to devise an assessment and place a child on a structured programme of teaching.

When learning, it is best if a teacher sticks to a recognised assessment, programme and sequence. Once a number of programmes and learners have been considered and progress made, a teacher may then feel competent to place a child or young person on their own carefully devised programme of teaching and learning.

Teaching should be systematic and cumulative, building on what has been learned and not assuming learning unless there has been specific teaching. Teaching is therefore organised in a way that follows the logical order of the language. Presentation of material is structured from the most basic and works through to the more complicated, bearing in mind also the usefulness of the various elements of language. For example, although the word 'the' is irregular, it is a very necessary element for learning language and must be taught early even though it is not phonically regular in its pronunciation. Teacher-learner interaction is promoted by the direct teaching of all concepts in a systematic and sequential order.

Close monitoring of progress is of course required to ensure mastery and automaticity before continuing on with the teaching programme. Progress is regularly measured to record improvement and to ensure this continues as is anticipated. **See Appendix 5 for ideas on how to record progress**.

The Alphabet Arc

The alphabet arc is an extremely useful tool that can help ensure that teaching points are multisensory. The letters can be either plastic or wooden. Any points to be taught can be planned so that in learning there is no fear of failure as learners can lay out the letters, swap them around if they make a mistake and the end product is always correct.

When laying out the arc, teachers often query whether learners should say the letter names or the sounds. As letters can make more than one sound, it is usually best to say the letter names for this task. Saying sounds in order doesn't generally come automatically and we want the alphabet to become automatic, so better stick to the letter names when laying out and teach the various sounds in the main part of the lesson.

Learners can see any mistakes they make and be guided to find the right solution. They say the letters (oral and aural), lay them out while saying the names (kinaesthetic), feel the letter shapes if desired (tactile), and then check (visual). Almost any points can be taught using the letters in the arc.

Sometimes spare letters are required and it is best if the teacher ensures there are plenty of the common letters available for use as and when required. Depending on the age and stage the learner is at additional multisensory work can be planned for when the letters are in use with an emphasis on structure, and ensuring learner participation and discovery learning ensuring students are facilitated to work out rules for themselves whenever possible.

It is useful to teach syllables and vowels very early in the teaching and explain to children why it is important to know which letters are vowels, and then recognise that there is one vowel (at least) in every syllable. Children must of course recognise that the letter 'y' sometimes behaves as a vowel and can make an /ĭ/ sound as it does in 'happy', and in 'spy' it makes an /ī/ sound. Building up this kind of information can impact positively on spelling though children will need lots of examples to give overlearning.

With the alphabet arc, it is useful to have cards with the breve and macron symbols handy so children can place these appropriately when making up words and learning the rules – for example, that at the end of a word, 'y' behaves as a vowel, but at the beginning it is a consonant and makes a /y/ sound.

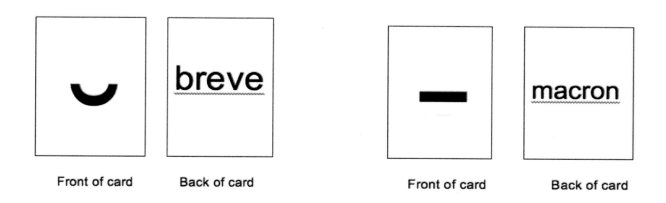

Front of card   Back of card   Front of card   Back of card

These cards can be placed above the vowels for teaching points such as doubling of consonants after a short vowel when adding –ed, -ing or -est endings. The student learns that when there is one consonant after a short vowel (as in 'stop'), the consonant has to be doubled to prevent –ing, -ed, or –est making the vowel say a long sound. The consonant blocks the vowel in, thus making it short. In 'stopped' the extra 'p' makes the letter 'o' short. It is good to demonstrate using wooden or plastic letters so learners can see how this happens. Learners can then show this by putting a breve on top of the letter when they write it so they come to understand how the rule works.

STŎP   S̶T̶Ŏ̶P̶E̶D̶ ✗   STŎPPED ✔

With only one 'p', the word says   STŌPED ✗

73

Placing letters out to form words in a few similar examples helps explain why there are double consonants in the middle of words such as stopped, clapping, hitting, fittest, sadder, summer, etc. There are a multitude of other teaching points that are facilitated by explanations involving short and long vowel sounds. These can be found in any good clearly structured phonic teaching programme. **See Appendix 2 - Structured Cumulative Multisensory Teaching Programmes.**

As an activity for putting the letters away instead of just reciting the letters, the student can be shown two letters on a card roughly 12 cm x 8 cm. Get her to say the next letter, then put away all three letters, so you say, for example:

MN _,
and your learner says, "MNO",
picks out MNO and puts away all three letters,
then select another card, perhaps ST_.
Student says, "STU", and puts the letters away.

You'll start with your pile of cards and show the student these one at a time. Then as a future activity, you can give a different set of cards with a different letter missing, so _EF, _KL with all the letters being included so you end up with the whole alphabet sequence being practised again in a different way.

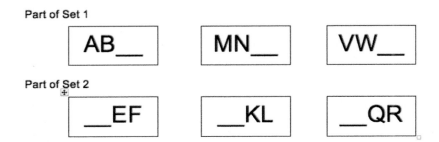

Add a set of cards which have the middle letter missing so that in all you will have at least three sets of cards, each set comprising the whole alphabet. This will give ample opportunity and practice with alphabet letters and gaining skills that will help in other areas when alphabetical order and sequencing are required.

The disadvantage of the method is that it really requires a one-to-one or very small group situation to be effective so it is not always appropriate in a classroom situation.

Chapter 7

Meeting Learners' Needs
in the Classroom

It is acknowledged that many children and young people with specific learning difficulties will benefit from individual teaching and support. However in classrooms it is not always possible or desirable to manage a number of different structured programmes, so in addition to the general help recommended earlier, consideration needs to be given to ways in which this can be managed.

> It is often possible to individualise teaching and learning so that the needs of individuals are met without the need for one-to-one individual teaching. This may entail bringing together children with other needs such as those learning English as an additional language or those with more general or other specific needs at some times.

It must not however be the norm that young people with specific learning needs are grouped together. Flexibility of teaching is absolutely essential if the learner with dyslexia as well as the other learners is to be accommodated appropriately and gain maximum benefit. It is also worth considering that there may be several young people in any classroom who will benefit from a highly structured teaching programme with multisensory methods to aid learning. Flexibility is however the key to the success of the teaching in mainstream classes.

SPECIFIC HELP IN VARIOUS AREAS OF THE CURRICULUM

The following is a brief selection of ideas that a teacher can use to help learners with specific learning difficulties to cope with the everyday curriculum. It also gives an indication of the areas that are likely to be affected. It must be stated that overlearning is necessary and much is left to the ingenuity of classroom teachers to devise strategies and techniques that are relevant, interesting and motivating to the class and learner.

LANGUAGE WORK

Reading

The process of learning to read is about bringing together various aspects of language:
- phonology - understanding of sounds
- syntax - how words and sentences work to produce meaning and be understood
- semantics – meaning
- morphology - how the little parts of words influence meaning
- orthography - how our understanding of letters and patterns of letters link to words and hence to the language system.

These aspects must then be related to the learners' background knowledge to form a circuit that brings all the processes together resulting in comprehension and an individual understanding of print. For the majority of children, the achievement of reading skills is a straightforward process and represents additional access to education. For those with dyslexia however the circuit does not work efficiently due to weakness in one or more aspects of the process.

Much of children's future learning will be determined by the level of their reading achievement. The world of books will help children discover their social and cultural backgrounds. In the early stages, reading will contribute to the further development of language. Through the related skills of handwriting and spelling they will acquire the ability to communicate and express themselves in written language – a skill that is usually readily transferable to modern technologies.

For most children reading is an easier process to master than spelling. This may be due to the fact that reading only requires the child to use recognition processes as opposed to the total recall of words. For reading it is sufficient for the child merely to recognise the word. She does not have to recall actual letters. In reading intelligent use of context is often helpful. This is not always the case in spelling. In reading too there is no necessity to remember patterns requiring motor skills as is required in writing out spellings. When a child who is otherwise 'normal' in his development fails to learn to read, it is a matter of considerable concern to both parents and teachers alike. What is required is a critical appraisal of why the methods already tried have failed to produce the desired results.

There is significant research evidence that suggests that training children to recognise alliteration and rhyme will help them develop reading and spelling skills. It is therefore useful to encourage all children to be aware of these features of language from an early age. To establish any children who may lack awareness of alliteration and rhyme invite them to find words that start with the same letter – e.g. clever, cunning, cool, cat. Children find as many words as possible. The same applies for rhyming words: my, fly, sly, spy. Children can also be asked to pick out a word which doesn't rhyme from a rhyming series – find the 'odd one out', so my, fly, sly, fat, magpie. This can form part of an early screening and intervention programme.

Lots of fun games can be devised to incorporate these principles and reinforce rhyming and alliteration skills from an early age – preferably pre-school. These skills can be reinforced at a slightly later stage by making the process more multisensory using plastic or wooden letters and exchanging a letter or two, so for example, pin, win, fin, spin. Children can then see (and say) the difference it makes when you insert a letter 'a' instead of 'i' for example.

From assessment it can be determined if there are memory difficulties that are hampering learning and affecting the learning of phonics, spelling, numeracy and organisation. There are many approaches that may be effective and it is worth trying more than one if the first is not as effective as we would like. As with all learning, the approaches should be multisensory and focused on making progress while maintaining a positive approach. However, not all approaches will use all of the senses all of the time, so we should not discard an approach just because of this.

Reading schemes are often based on a combined phonic and look-and-say approach. Many children with specific learning difficulties do succeed in achieving a reasonable degree of proficiency using this approach if they are of good ability level but this is not always the case.

When children with dyslexia do succeed in reaching a reasonable degree of proficiency they are generally relying on areas of strength to compensate for the weaker areas.

For example, a child who is a good visualiser may achieve success through recognition of word shapes and patterns, and also may be able to make good use of context clues. The child who has a poor visual memory, but is good at 'sounding out', may also achieve a relative amount of success through ability to memorise sounds auditorily. When unable to 'sound out', she too may make use of context. Seldom however do these learners reach a level commensurate with their ability, and reading is often seen as a chore to be tolerated in the school context but seldom enjoyed.

The skill of reading is a highly complex mental process involving not only the recognition of letters and patterns, but also the interaction of context and meaning with visual and auditory information. A learner with dyslexia needs a structured cumulative approach in which reading, writing and spelling are integrated. Reading skill is gained by systematically building up letter sounds into syllables, then into words. From words, the child progresses to sentences and to continuous prose. Practice must be frequent and regular. Materials used must be structured in such a way that the child can progress in a logical, step-by-step fashion with continuous monitoring of progress. Suggestions for structured programmes are given in Appendix 2. Some have been around for many years and some are new. Older programmes such as Letterland have proved themselves over the years, but some of the new programmes may be equally or more effective.

Letterland, for younger children in particular, provides attractively presented material in a well-structured way which the children find entertaining and extremely beneficial. The system has been kept updated and introduces pictograms as mapping devices that help children to identify and differentiate between similar letter shapes (b/d/p/q, s/z, u/n, H/N, M/W etc). Initially the names of the Letterland characters, like the Hairy Hat Man (h) provide a shape/sound mnemonic for each letter, accompanied by a little story explanation. The children have fun drawing and illustrating the phonic points made by the programme.

Hairy Hat Man - Letterland

The previous illustration of a child's drawings shows how the child has built on her previously learnt knowledge of single sounds and stories to learn new sounds, such as /sh/. For example, the 'sh' story in brief:

Sammy Snake (s) loves to hiss, but the Hairy Hat Man (h) hates noise, so the Hairy Hat Man hushes up Sammy Snake whenever they are next to each other in a word, saying /sh/ ....!

Each story acts as an aide memoire helping the children to recall pattern, sequence and sound. The examples above show how the children can also 'vitalise' the letters themselves and picture code them in words where the sound occurs making learning a fun experience. A range of backup materials exist for most of the phonics programmes on the market, making the teachers' job and record keeping straightforward, and providing a range of material to support reinforcement and overlearning – computer software, films, games, planning and assessment materials.

It is for teachers to determine what will best suit their learners, but the principles of being highly structured, cumulative and multisensory apply. Programmes can sometimes be amalgamated to provide the best approach for the children.

One aim of these structured multisensory programmes is to get the learner to form an automatic response between visually presented letter patterns and units of sound, e.g. 't-i-o-n' says /sh'n/. The learner must realise that to sound out individual letters in such cases is of no help in pronouncing the word. With daily practice conducted in a multisensory way, responses should in time become automatic. Stick to around five phonemes at a time until these have been mastered. The more attractive the material presented, the more likely the learner is to enjoy what she is doing and to gain maximum benefit from it. For younger children in particular the learning must be fun as well as being well structured and multisensory

The main problem in managing these programmes for the teacher is how such schemes can be operated within the classroom situation when the rest of the class have reached a point when they no longer require specific phonic training. Looking realistically, it will be difficult for the class teacher to find the necessary time to spend practising with one individual unless some extra provision is made for this. We have to look at an approach that will suit a group either within the classroom or if different classes could be organised. This is obviously much easier to arrange on a regular basis where a support teacher or specialist is involved.

In grouping children we have to bear in mind that the child with dyslexia does not lack capacity and that their reading problems are in processing symbolic information, not in understanding meaning. If the child is grouped with others who have more general learning difficulties for phonic work, she will feel very much aware of this fact, so we must make sure she is placed with children of similar interest and ability levels for other areas of the curriculum.

Though it can never be a substitute for good empathic teaching, technology can be very useful in reinforcing skills and giving the much needed overlearning and patient practice that children with dyslexia need. Resources such as Nessy and Floppy's Phonics Sounds and Letters provide the busy teacher with resources which children can use with a teaching assistant or in a small group. These programs give repeated presentations of material to help the children gain automaticity in responding to words and sounds, and then starting to make sense of what they've read.

However, if children have started to learn phonics using these resources and are still struggling at later stages when we'd expect them to have mastered phonics and reading, then a fresh resource will be better than toiling with a tool which children know has already resulted in failure and ceased to maintain their interest.

It is important that the young people have enthusiasm for their learning and that this can be maintained for a sustained period so that progress can be seen by the teacher and felt by the learner. Learners with dyslexia benefit from high interest reading material at a level that they can read and enjoy. Similarly with computer software and apps we must look at the interest level as well as the reading level and ensure the material appeals to the learners involved.

Nessy Phonics   -   **Floppy Phonics**, Oxford Univ. Press

Once children are progressing through the phonemes, they should be taught syllabification to learn how to break words into their constituent parts. This will aid both reading and spelling. Affixes should be taught as such and the child encouraged to consider which part of a word is the root, the prefix or suffix. Children who are interested can also be taught the derivation of the various parts of the word. **See later section on Morphology**.

In teaching word attack skills then the following pattern should ensure an adequate progression provided the child has adequate experience of all the processes.

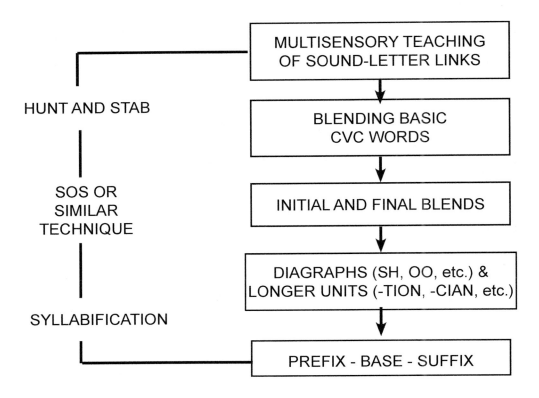

In the case of difficult or irregular words where these can readily be matched to pictures, matching games like Pelmanism can be played. Another technique for recognition and recall of irregular words could be through using a Hunt and Stab technique.

For the **Hunt and Stab** technique:

1. Choose the necessary irregular words (e.g. from a page of the child's reading book).
2. Put each of the words on a separate, small card and read the words along with the child.
3. Ask the child to identify a specific word – e.g. "See if you can find me the word," 'enough'. Encourage the child to look at initial letters where these will help – HUNT AND STAB!
4. Form the words into a column, and invite the child to try to remember each one.
5. Make a separate column of all the words remembered and congratulate the child on these.

This technique will help the child recognise the words but will probably have very little carry-over to spelling. For this, and for the remaining words that are posing a recognition problem, the child could employ the SOS technique **described in the Spelling section**.

Encourage children to look for patterns in a word and show how they can use this to help work out how to pronounce the word. This is necessary for children to be able to divide words into syllables to aid word recognition skills: e.g. in the word 'rabbit', children should learn to divide the word between the two 'b's in such a way that they will recognise that they have two closed syllables and hence two short vowels (răb /bĭt). Similarly children should look out for regular final syllables such as 'ble', 'stle', 'tion' etc.

In a holistic model of reading, there can be no one method of instruction but a selection of means to achieve the ends. While structured multisensory practice of phonemes on a daily basis will help give instant recognition of letter patterns, the child can also gain much from having stories read. Also, listening to recordings of books, while at the same time following the story, is useful.

Paired reading, either with a good reader or parents, can be encouraged to give children and young people much of the pleasure of books which they are losing because of their difficulties. There is a great deal of evidence that the involvement of parents in both paired and shared reading can be highly beneficial. **See paired reading on the CD**. If parents are themselves non-readers, then there needs to be discussion with them so that reading with someone at home can be encouraged. For example, neighbours, grandparents, volunteers can sometimes fill this gap. There should be no shame in disclosing reading difficulties and parents too can benefit from becoming involved in listening to books that have been downloaded or streamed and sharing in discussing these with their children.

Morphology

Morphemes are the smallest meaningful units of language and cannot be subdivided into smaller meaningful parts. Morphology considers how morphemes are structured and how words are formed in language. It looks at the roots of language and analyses how words can change through bringing together the various parts, such as the root word, prefixes and suffixes. Awareness of how words are formed can help children to understand the meaning of the word. It can also help with spelling, as there are often rules that have to be followed in relation to adding prefixes and suffixes for example.

To help the child to 'sound out' words he is unsure of, he is taught how to break words into their constituent parts. In multisyllabic words the child should be encouraged to consider which part of a word is the root, the prefix and the suffix. The child with average to high ability will appreciate a morphological approach once initial sounds and phonics have been mastered.

Just as becoming phonologically aware is an essential skill for learners with dyslexia, so morphological awareness can assist students' learning to read, write and spell. Morphology has for a long time been overlooked in the early years of school and been assigned for later stages. It is now appreciated that it has its place throughout and can benefit the early stages of learning as much if not more than later. It is helpful too for anyone who finds literacy difficult – helping as it does, breaking down words into their constituent parts, and building up words and giving meaning or changing meaning depending on what we add or take away.

If young people learn how to marry phonological skills with orthographic and morphological skills, the three can work in harmony and give multi-sensory practice in a meaningful way.

> Once students have built morphological skills, they can break words down and predict meaning from the parts of the word so a word such as 'unkind' can be used to establish that the morpheme 'un' means 'not'. Once specific morphemic units are known and understood, learners can break down and make up words and understand their meanings and how these came about.

Young children use inflectional morphemes such as 's', 'ed', 'ing' (packs, packed, packing) without much thought and morphological production will generally be in place prior to school entry though not every inflectional morpheme is regular in the same way. Derivational morphemes (useful, teacher, unclear) which change meaning to a greater extent may require more thought but be more helpful to the child's developing language and knowledge. For example if the child learns that '–ess' means female, and already knows the word 'princess' then this will lead to the knowledge of the meaning of priestess, hostess, governess and also that these words all have a double 's' at the end.

There is evidence that some children pick up morphological awareness just as they pick up phonological awareness. Others need systematic teaching to benefit from the knowledge this can bring. There are various activities and games that can be introduced as well as direct teaching. Initially some systematic teaching will help learners become aware of roots, prefixes and suffixes. For example, the teacher might introduce the root 'act' and tell the students that this means 'do'. 'Re' means 'again', 'inter' means 'between' or 'among'. That may be enough for one teaching session depending on the age and stage of the children. The children can work out the new word meanings, and then write the words in a word book specially kept for their morphology lessons. Gradually suffixes are introduced too, or some of the most common ones can be interspersed initially and others added later.

Teachers, or the children themselves, can put the root words onto card with prefixes and suffixes also on card and use these to build words. They might for example have the root 'act' on a card, then take an 'or' suffix, a 're' prefix, and build words with the challenge of working out the meanings of the new words they have just built. Ensure the roots, suffixes and prefixes are colour coded as some morphemes (such as 'en' can be both a suffix and a prefix). If for example all the roots are in red, the prefixes in yellow and the suffixes in green, then it's clear whether learners are working with a prefix, a suffix or a root word. It's helpful also if the meaning of the morpheme is included on the back of the card with some words which illustrate the morpheme there too.

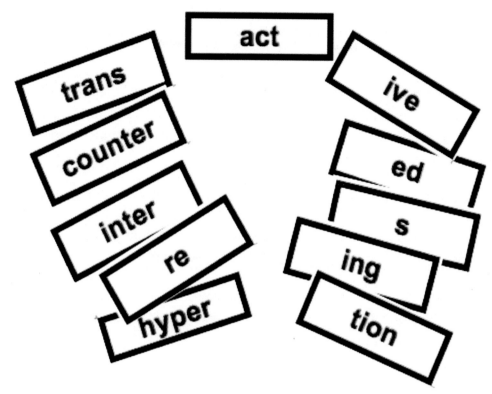

Sample of the front of cards for morphological awareness

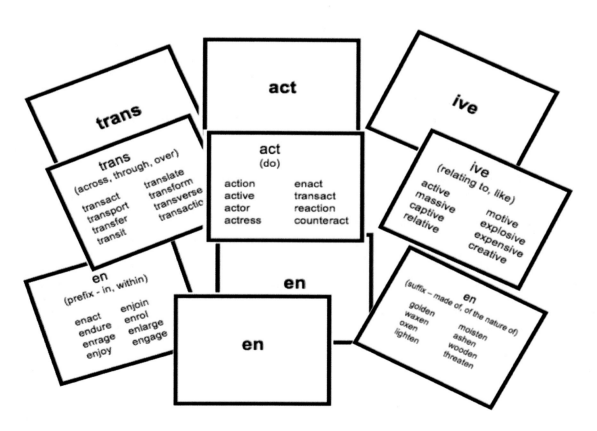

Front and back of cards for morphological awareness

Some activities to give practice:

- **Snap – match a root word and a prefix**. If the two don't make a larger word then they are not a match.

- **How many words can you think of which end with the suffix ….** for example, 'ful'. This gives the opportunity to reinforce the spelling of 'ful' as a suffix, and 'full' when it's a word on its own. If students are still at an early stage in learning about morphology, then choose easy suffixes – 'ment', 'less', 'ing' etc.

- **Spot the root word in …..** helpful, mindless, bending, reactive, revisit, description etc.

- From a number of cards spread out on the table, find the common root. Learners have to find words and match the cards that have the same root word.

- Bingo. The caller calls a root from a deck of root words. The players have cards with prefixes and suffixes on them. The players must make a real word, so if the caller calls 'late,' the player can put a marker over 'trans' –prefix (translate) or 'ly' – suffix (lately) for example. When Bingo is called the others help check if all the words are real words.

- For word building, allow the learner to use Lego bricks or similar construction material, and use sticky-backed Velcro to tape root words, prefixes and suffixes onto these. The learner then builds whole words from these and works out the meanings. The learner says the word as he builds it, making the activity multisensory.

  The use of Velcro and laminated cards means that the same Lego bricks can be used and the cards can be swapped to suit the teaching point that is being supported. This activity can also be used for word and sentence building at various stages as a fun way to reinforce teaching points.

- Once a reasonable selection of prefix, suffix and root cards have been accumulated, lay these on the table, and get children to find how many new words they can make. Write them down. They can use a mini white board for this so any errors can be quickly sorted.

Make the activities as multisensory as you can so the learners see, visualise, hear, speak out (or sub-vocalise if it is not appropriate to say aloud) and write the words they make. Some of the activities can be timed activities – students are given one minute to find, or think of, or write the answers. This will depend on the nature of the group which is doing the activity. If you are always going to have one in the group who is last, this will not serve to motivate, and that student will not benefit.

Opportunities must be taken to relate the language being introduced to particular areas of the curriculum or to topics being covered, or to the reading books or whatever. Students must see it as relevant in order to find it helpful. There need to be repeated opportunities for practice of vocabulary and reinforcement of meanings in a purposeful way. When tied with phonological awareness, sound and letter patterns can be married and related to spelling so the student can identify patterns and regularities. Activities need to be motivating and encourage students to become more independent in working out meanings and spellings for themselves.

Morphological awareness practice can be a good supplement to other multisensory phonics teaching, and where phonic approaches have previously resulted in disillusionment, can provide a fresh and novel approach with beneficial results in terms of vocabulary understanding and spelling. It can provide another useful teaching approach when it is done systematically and explicitly.

On its own morphological awareness can offer a way forward but the approach needs to be fun and appeal to the learners. There needs to be direct teaching of root words, their meanings and how these blend with various affixes to make new and interesting words. Teachers therefore need to ensure that they have a good knowledge of morphology in order that they can pass their knowledge on.

In all activities connected to the reading process, adequate practice is vital to develop efficient memorisation and automatisation. At all times due regard must be given to the learners' opinion on what they like or don't like. For this reason they must be motivated by the self-improving and self-rewarding nature of reading. It is critical therefore that the teachers accept responsibility for providing stimulating and interesting material that is at an appropriate level and stage for the needs of the individual.

Some suggestions are made in **Appendix 2** for material that can be used with children with specific difficulties and also for older children with dyslexia who would be insulted by the initial stages of infant reading schemes. At all stages, the teacher must be guided by the child. If a child dislikes a series of books sufficiently, she is unlikely to learn much from them. Try to find a series that appeals, and then encourage activities that will sustain interest throughout.

Once the child is decoding words at a reasonably efficient level, the aim will be to improve skills of comprehension, accuracy and speed. There is an interrelationship between these skills and it will be difficult for a learner to increase comprehension while fluency and accuracy are still weak. Misreading a single word at the start of a passage or book can throw the reader off course, and lead to misunderstanding of the whole passage or much of the book.

There are different ways of improving the skills involved in reading.

For speed and accuracy:

1. Computer games can be fun and motivating and can help build up confidence.

2. Audacity is a free open source digital software application that can be used for recording and editing sound and speech. Using Audacity, let the learner record herself reading a familiar passage – from her reading book or other familiar material. When she has finished reading the passage, place an acetate sheet over the book for the child to mark so the book doesn't get damaged. The learner goes back and listens and carefully and marks any errors by underlining the word on the acetate with an erasable marking pen. The child may need some help to begin this.

   She then plays back the recording from the start, again following carefully. When she comes to the first wrong word, she starts to record again, pronouncing the word correctly and reading on with the rest of the story. She is aiming to finish more quickly than the previous time.

   Children can do this a few times ensuring there are no more errors. The aim is of course to improve accuracy and speed. The teacher will need to supervise to ensure the children can spot their own mistakes.

3. Many children with dyslexia read little words wrongly even after they are able to pronounce the larger words. This can be due to concentrating hard on the apparently more difficult big words at the expense of the seemingly easy little ones. To help children become aware of this and increase automaticity and accuracy, two children with equivalent reading levels can work together trying to spot one another's errors with little words. Again an acetate placed over the reading book can be used. Don't worry about the big words at this point and only mark the words the children know they should be getting right.

   Each child starts with 10 points and loses a point each time they make an error with words such as 'a', 'the', 'for', 'from' etc. For this to be successful it must be fun but it does help children become aware of having to focus on the little words as well as the large ones. The children aim to get a higher score each time they read a passage of equivalent length.

For comprehension:

4. Prepare vocabulary and information about the content of a passage before students start to read. If learners have background knowledge and understand some of the vocabulary that will be used, they will not need to rely on decoding to such a great extent.

5. For students who are weak readers, give them access to a digital version of the text in preparation for later reading and discussion. If students have the text and can follow a digital recording of the content, they will get much more out of the story or information that will follow. This can be made available to all through the school website, but the students with dyslexia are likely to gain maximum benefit. Care does need to be taken not to infringe copyright.

6. If students are particularly weak in accessing text, then a digital reader on the computer is likely to be of benefit. Speech can readily be enabled on most modern computers, tablets and held-held devices or students can use text-to-speech software.

7. To help with comprehension a 'reciprocal teaching' (sometimes called 'reciprocal reading') approach can be taken. This involves working with children in a group situation. It involves four main processes first noted in a study by Palincsar and Brown (1986) with a high rate of success:

    *   Summarising
    *   Questioning
    *   Clarifying
    *   Predicting.

To start, the teacher provides a model for the young people to follow, and begins by reading the title and inviting predictions about the content that is to follow, then reads the first paragraph. Summarising is modelled as a self-review activity. If an adequate synopsis cannot be reached, this is not regarded as a failure but as a source of information that comprehension is not occurring and activities such as rereading or clarifying are needed. Questioning is a goal (not an isolated activity) - what was the main idea, what happened then, why etc? Working with the young people, the teacher then clarifies. If there is confusion of any kind (either in the text or in the student's interpretation), this is discussed.

Prediction is then attempted. Students and the teacher look for cues that serve to herald forthcoming material. This is all undertaken as part of the actual reading.
Once the students have established a good model, then one of the students can take the role of the teacher and lead the reading and discussion. If one student is a particularly weak reader then it is sufficient for them to read in a paired reading manner supported by a partner or the whole group. In this way, students are able to take part in the activity at their own level of understanding.

If the group comprises reasonably capable readers, then the reading can be done silently a paragraph at a time once the technique is established. The teacher maintains the role of teacher and stays in charge until the young people get the idea of what they are to do. The teacher continues to provide support and appropriate encouragement and praise throughout.

There are various adaptations of this activity that have been developed. It is important to ensure that the activities are appropriate for the group of children involved.

8 Visualising the content of a passage is another helpful approach that can greatly improve comprehension and interest. This must be led by the teacher to start. To begin, a paragraph is chosen where there is a good amount of visual imagery. A sentence or two are chosen to start, and then the teacher leads the discussion. This is dependent on the content, but if we suppose a 'house' is mentioned in the first sentence. The apprentice readers are asked to tell the teacher about the house – What's it like? What size is it? Is it an old or a new house? How many windows? Where is the door? Are there curtains on the windows? What is the roof like? What is the weather like when you see this house in your mind? Does the house have a garden? etc.

If certain features are not mentioned in the story, then the visual image created by the children will be just as valid as if they had been mentioned. What is important is that the children form an image in their minds as an aid to memory. It can be useful at a later stage for children to discuss the different pictures that they have created in their minds and why some might be more relevant than others. To start with however it is probably best to stick to one visual image at a time.

The teacher continues to ask questions focusing on one child to begin with and the picture of the house that they have visualised. Once the child has created a good image for the teacher, the teacher praises the young person and tells the group that he has a good picture of the house now, and the teacher then moves on to the next sentence (or item that can be visualised).

The whole process is led by the teacher until the group have grasped how visualisation works. The learner can then ask the teacher or choose another member of the group to create the imagery. In this way, the children learn to create their own visual imagery of the content of a passage, and then of a whole story, thus improving comprehension and memory.

Though this process is time consuming to start with, once the young people learn how to visualise and start to do this for themselves, the teacher can gradually reduce their support and feel confident that the young people are visualising for themselves. Though intended to increase comprehension for reading I have found this also helps writing in that young people start to produce much more descriptive and interesting pieces of written work.

Spelling

It is said that 'spelling is the tool of writing'. The purpose of children being taught to spell is that they may become fluent in written language. The goal in teaching spelling is therefore not for belaboured accuracy, but to encourage spelling to become an automatic process. When children have dyslexia, the acquisition of spelling patterns in response to spoken language does not take place as a matter of course. Considerable effort on the part of both the teacher and the learner is required, and much overlearning on the part of the child must take place before a word will become known.

> When specific learning difficulties are severe, we must accept the fact that some children will never become perfect spellers for every occasion. An aim for these children is to give them spelling strategies to enable fluency in writing words and sufficiently logical spelling that their work will be easily understood by all who read it.

Technology can help compensate for inaccuracies so belabouring spelling may not in the long run be worth the effort. If spelling becomes reasonably accurate and the young person is encouraged to use a word processor then often the computer will correct the spelling resulting in a very acceptable piece of work. Students will need not only to be taught to use existing tools such as spell-checkers but also newer tools such as AutoCorrect where writers create a list of commonly misspelt words and their correct spellings and the word processor automatically converts the misspelling - for example, if 'accommodate' is a much used word then it could be listed with 'acommodate', 'accomodate' and 'accommodate', and the computer would automatically correct the wrong versions.

While children are happy to work on spelling and benefiting, continuing the teaching of spelling will be appropriate. In teaching spelling multisensory methods are again advocated. The learner should hear the sound or word she has to spell, say the sound or word, spell it, write it, look at it and check the spelling. The technique for SOS described later in this section employs multisensory methods in this way. The Look, (Say), Cover, Write and Check routine is also described and can be used in a multisensory way.

For a learner who has reasonable underlying ability there is no reason why spelling rules should not be taught. In fact, it is advocated that they should be. To do this in school, class teachers must make sure they are acquainted with the rules before teaching them to the children. There are several books as well as Internet resources that can help with this. **See Appendix 2**. If we are to cover all the main rules these rules must be taught in a logical order, so check if there is a book or online source available so you don't have to organise these for yourself. We must of course record the child's progress so that we know exactly what has been taught and when, so that any other teacher can take over if necessary and complete the programme. Ideally we would follow a similar structure for spelling to that in use for phonics. If spelling is practised and checked daily, this encourages spelling to become the automatic process for which we are aiming.

Spelling should follow the sequence of:

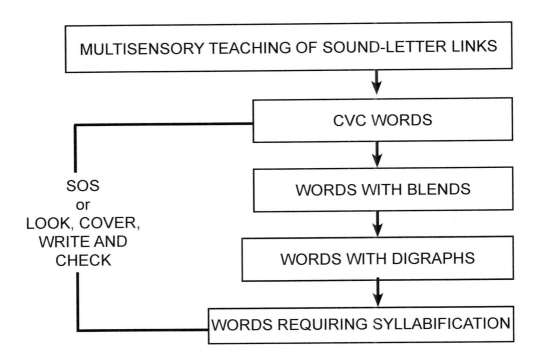

Teach:

1. Groups of words which rhyme, e.g. 'send', 'mend', 'spend'

2. Sound patterns and digraphs, e.g. 'ee', 'al', 'est', 'igh'

3. Rules, guidelines and regularities
   When there is no actual rule which applies and the learner is uncertain about spelling, the learner should learn to apply certain guidelines, such as 'For an /ē/ sound in the middle of a one-syllable word, use double e'. This may not always be right but it does at least give the most likely option.

4. Alongside enabling the learner to relate spelling patterns to sounds, much rich information can be gained from discussing derivations, functions and meanings of words. Looking at the roots of words can enable the learner to see why homonyms are represented differently in spelling: e.g. eight (number 8) and ate (past tense of the verb eat). Teaching morphological awareness as discussed previously will also help with spelling.

5. Prefixes and suffixes should be considered for the meaning that is conveyed through them. Instead of regarding English words as "just plain stupid", the learner will see the logic of spelling words differently to differentiate meaning. For the older child, recognising the relationships between words such as statistician and statistics will help the young person to realise why we use the spelling statistician, not statistition.

Unless one-to-one teaching is available from a specialist, the class teacher may find it difficult to justify the time spent with one individual. However, it may be quite possible to establish a group of students who could benefit from such methods. This may or may not be the same grouping as for reading. Examples of suitable schemes for spelling are given in **Appendix 2. See also section on Morphology**.

6. The Simultaneous Oral Spelling technique (SOS), first introduced by Gillingham and Stillman, is multisensory and has proved highly successful. The procedure for this is:

   i.   Words to be learned are presented one at time, each on a small card. Alternatively, make up the word with the child, using wooden or plastic letters.
   ii.   The teacher reads the word and the child repeats it.
   iii. The child then writes the word, saying the name of each letter as it is written, repeating the word.
   iv.   The child then checks back to the original to ensure the word is correct.
   v.   The word is covered and the process is repeated twice more.

If the word is practised three times a day for five or six days using this technique, it may well succeed when other methods have failed. To reduce the load on memory the word should be related to others that have the same pattern and sound - count, mount, fount; sound, bound, found, mound, pound, round, wound. Try to elicit as much as you can from the learner to give greater ownership of the learning. Once they realise there is often a pattern to be found, this does help.

The LOOK, COVER, WRITE and CHECK routine is very similar. To gain maximum benefit, the child requires to attend to a few additional factors when employing this technique.

LOOK: Learners should say out the spelling of the word while at the same time looking at it. They may require to spell it out several times while at the same time trying to visualise the pattern. Only when they think they can remember the word should they continue to the next stage.

COVER: The word is covered so it cannot be seen.

WRITE: The word is then written from memory, again saying the spelling while at the same time writing.

CHECK: Check carefully by spelling out the original while looking at both the original and the newly written version. If the word is wrong, go back and repeat the process.

The word should be practised a few times and the child should come back to it again at regular intervals until it is firmly established.

Whatever the age and stage of the learner, the emphasis is as always on the use of multisensory methods when practising spelling, and in building up the learner's spelling vocabulary in a structured and cumulative manner. While explaining the logic behind spelling will help, it is insufficient on its own.

> The essentials when practising spelling words are that learners must see the word, say the word, spell out the letters in the word, then look and check that the word is correct. They must learn to monitor their own spelling and look carefully for any mistakes, so that constant dependence on the teacher will gradually diminish.

Visual Tracking

Another strategy that can help spelling and also encourage learners to track along lines carefully from left to right is to prepare worksheets for specific topic work or for individuals' specific spelling weaknesses, subject-specific vocabulary, etc. Prepare a worksheet similar to the one below with the target word written at the top, and then embedded in the print below. This is for a student who often mis-spells the word 'with', often writing 'whith' or 'whit' instead of 'with'. The student tracks along from left to right and when he sees the correct order of letters, he says "doubleyou, eye, tee, aitch – with", and circles the word each time he finds the embedded word.

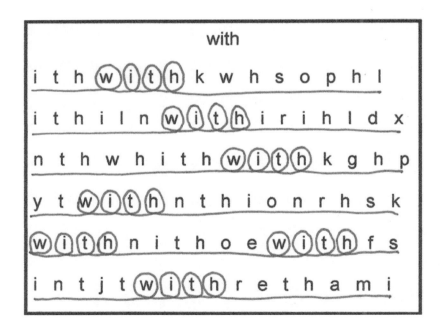

Mnemonics

Silly or ridiculous sentences e.g. "A bright light might give me a slight fright at night" (for words with 'ight') can be used to emphasise a specific (in this case, rhyming) pattern and act as an aid to memory. The use of mnemonic strategies as an aide-memoire is often effective for the child who is unable to visualise the pattern of a word, but has sufficient auditory memory skill to memorise mnemonics. The more ridiculous the mnemonics, the more likely they are to be remembered, e.g. "Some Nuns Run Very Well" may help the child to remember to use –el instead of 'le' at the end of words after s, n, r, v and w – tunnel, not tunnle. This in addition to a pictorial representation may be even more useful.

A man with too MANY heads   A CLOWN with a FROWN and a CROWN

In this example the child was looking for a way to remember the spelling of the word 'many'. Seeing the word 'man' in 'many' helped.

The clown example reinforces the 'ow' pattern that comes before the letter 'n' when making the /ow/ sound. There is then no confusion on whether to write 'ou', so avoiding the possibility of 'cloun', 'froun, or 'croun'.

Children can be good at thinking up their own mnemonic strategies if encouraged to do so.   If they put their drawings and spellings onto a pack of small cards, both teacher and pupil can see the reasoning behind the strategy and ensure that this is sound.

Visualisation

This is a very useful strategy – particularly helpful if you have a learner with visual strengths, but even if the learner is not strong visually, it may be useful. The technique can be learned. You can start by using the approach for learning spelling, but the strategy will work for numbers (PIN numbers, phone numbers, etc.) and can be extended to any area of life.
Use the following procedure:

a) Write what has to be learned in large clear print (word with correct spelling, number sequence, formula or whatever on a flip chart, white board, or something large). Use a broad felt tip pen or bold font if on a screen. Get the learner to look at it, then say it out loud to you. Can they remember it (spelling or whatever)? Get them to visualise it (look at it till it seems fixed in their mind). Then close eyes and still see it. Look at a blank bit of wall up to the left. Can they still remember it? If not, then look back until they think they can see it in their mind, and keep doing this till it seems fixed.

b) Get the learner to focus on a piece of blank wall, the same bit of wall as before, preferably looking up to their left. Can they still see it? Again if the answer is no, then they look back until they can. When they can you start to work with them on it. What is the first letter? What is the last letter?

c) Consider the part of the word they are finding tricky – maybe the 'p', 'h' in the middle of 'graphic' - so work through the word, starting, "What letter does the word 'graphic' start with, what follows the gee? That's right, it's the letter 'r'. What comes after the 'r'? That's right, it's an 'a'. Then ask "What are the two letters after the 'a'? That's right, pee, aitch". Now ask what colour these letters are. It doesn't matter what colour they say and it doesn't have to be the same as it was written. It's what is in their mind's eye that is important.

d) "Now look at this pee, aitch. You said it was green (or whatever they said). That's great! Now change the colour. Make it red! Can you see the pee, aitch in red? Now make the pee, aitch flash in red. Can you see it flashing?"

e) Continue to work through the word, but still go back to the flashing pee, aitch in the middle till you feel sure they've fully understood and got a clear picture in their mind.

f) Once they have worked their way through the word and you are satisfied they've understood the tricky part, then get them to look again so they can't see the original. Look at that bit of wall up there. Do they see the word?

g) Spell the word backwards.

h) Spell the word the right way now.

i)   Explain that you didn't really want them to learn to spell the word backwards, but that they just proved they can see the word in their mind and can now spell it! Finally spell it the right way once again.

This process is time-consuming when you start but once the technique is learned students can practise it for themselves and it does work for many of our students with lasting impact.

Dictionaries

Dictionary use should be encouraged too, but not always when the student is in the process of story writing as this may inhibit the flow of writing. In this case it may be better to come back at the end of the story and check through, looking out for doubtful words and checking with the dictionary. If the child is still making huge numbers of spelling errors, then it would be sufficient for him to check out just a few of the most common spelling mistakes. It is a good idea for the child to make his own pocketsize spelling dictionary of words that he frequently misspells, so that he can consult it regularly to check his spelling. If the child is unable to spot any likely mistakes on his own, then he may need a little guidance. Examples of the types of dictionary are given in Appendix 2. It is for the teacher to provide alternatives and for the learner to decide which he finds most suitable. However the teacher must try to retain a balance between the time spent and the value obtained if the student can learn to use the technology instead to ensure accuracy.

Digital dictionaries

There are several digital dictionaries available on the market that are designed to help anyone with a spelling difficulty. These are extremely portable and can be carried easily in a pocket or schoolbag. If these work well for individual learners then it is worth spending the money. However a good word processor will include the facility to check spelling and also the meaning of words without having to use a separate tool. There is sometimes a facility to create a bank of words for personalised vocabulary designed to match the curriculum of the student.   If considering a digital dictionary, it will be worth arranging to trial it before deciding to purchase as the integrated spelling checker and thesaurus in most current word processing packages is often enough.

A major benefit of ensuring a spelling checker is in use with whatever word processor is being used is that students know which words they can leave alone.

> A difficulty that people with dyslexia often face is that when they look at words,
> sometimes a word may look as if it's wrong when in fact it is right. This is probably
> due to them writing the word wrongly on previous occasions and that word then
> being held in memory.

Cued spelling

This strategy is based on the work of Keith Topping though there are undoubtedly others who have developed very similar approaches. The method has been evaluated and found to work well with students as young as seven. However it is also a very useful approach for older learners who have made only limited progress previously. Students however must be sensitively approached if this technique is to work. A good speller is paired with a weaker speller. This can be done with a few children from within a class but similarly it could be done with senior students paired with younger ones, or a parent with a child. It does have to be done one-to-one and is an equivalent approach for spelling as paired reading is for reading – it works well with non-professionals.

Firstly appropriate words are selected. These can be from a specific programme, subject-specific vocabulary or simply words that the young person has difficulty with and wants to be able to spell. Ideally cued spelling sessions last around fifteen minutes and happen about three times per week for an initial trial period of around six weeks.

Once the spelling has been checked, the word is written out and the learner and tutor read the word together, then the learner reads it alone. Between them they choose a cue that will aid memory. Though the tutor may make suggestions as to the most appropriate cue, the final decision lies with the learner. Cues can be phonic, mnemonic, chunking or any other or idiosyncratic strategy. They say the cue together. The learner then says the cue on her own and then the tutor writes the word. The tutor says the cue and the speller writes the word. The speller then says the cue and writes the word. The speller writes the word fast and reads the word. When the learner is writing the word, the tutor must ensure that the word is covered and the learner doesn't see it. If a word is written wrongly by the speller, then she has to cross it out quite deliberately, so it is crossed from memory.

The tutor has to remember to cover previous efforts. The speller has to check her own tries. If the word is wrongly spelled, they both go back to the previous step. The tutor gives lots of praise when the learner gets the cues and the spelling correct or if she spots her own errors without help. If the speller is unable to check her work accurately, help may be required from the tutor.

At the end of the session the speller writes out all the words she has learned that day and spells them fast. This can be between three and six words. If there is an error the steps are repeated. It is useful to have a mastery review each week to ensure spellings are retained. The pair must decide what they do about any errors that are found and keep a record of each day's score. If there are lots of errors and the learner is not enjoying the sessions, then after the six weeks it is likely the pair will decide to try something completely different.

Prompt spelling

The Prompt spelling approach promoted by Watkins and Hunter-Carsch takes advantage of many of the features of Cued Spelling. Each session is fairly short (15-20 minutes) and it too involves paired work with a tutor or 'prompter'. Here too the prompter can be a peer who is a good speller, an older student or parent. Before starting it is good to draw up several worksheets or a notebook with pages lined off in four columns.

The prompter begins by underlining four reasonably important words which the student has mis-spelled in a piece of work and these mis-spelt words are copied onto a prepared worksheet containing four vertical columns.

Each mis-spelling is discussed (phonically, letter patterns, spelling rules, etc). The prompter says the word clearly, enunciating all the syllables and stressing the part the learner got wrong. The learner repeats the word in a similar style.

The learner underlines the part of the word that he thinks is wrong and says why he thinks this way, and this is then discussed and the learner spells out his best effort.

Using a spell-checking device or dictionary, the word is checked and the correct spelling is put in Column 2 of the worksheet. Both look back at the first column and discuss why the first effort is wrong (bringing in phonics, spelling rules, syllables, morphology, etc).

The speller and prompter discuss similar words with same pattern and consider how and why they are similar. These are put in the third column.

The word that had the original error is then written correctly in the last column with the student spelling out the word as he writes and checking back with the correct version. This approach should be continued for as long as both the learner and the tutor feel that benefit is being gained. A sample worksheet is included on the CD with this book.

Very often young people with dyslexia spell a word differently at different parts of a piece of writing. Sometimes teachers find it difficult to understand why they get the word right at some points and wrong at others. The reason is generally that they don't know when it is right. This is perhaps the reason the paired sessions are effective. With a little help, the learner with dyslexia can be encouraged to leave alone the words that are correct and only tackle those with errors.

All of the approaches mentioned above may not work equally well so it is for the teacher to determine which method is most effective and stick with it for as long as appropriate. If the child gets easily bored and/or the learning is no longer effective, it is time to stop and consider a different approach or a different mix of approaches.

Correcting spelling in written work

When the learner is satisfied with his efforts, the teacher can then go over the work with him. In correcting the learner's work it is far better not to mark over his writing. It is less demoralising for the child if we have a system of writing the word correctly in the margin and allow the child to correct the mistakes himself.

When formal spelling is given, the teacher must decide the appropriate number of words to be practised at a time. For the younger child three or four are likely to be sufficient. Words with the same phonic point can be chosen as a group or family. Words which have similar sounds but which do not follow the rule being taught, should be treated as irregular words, e.g. when teaching the rule that 'll' is used for an /l/ sound at the end of a one syllable word after a short vowel, teach the word 'pal' as irregular. The child can then practise that word using the multisensory technique described before. When setting spelling homework for children with dyslexia, it is best to set only words which have previously been taught or for which the particular phonic point has been taught. Homework is then being used as a technique for reinforcement of the teaching points. It should not be a substitute.

When testing words to establish if the child has retained them, check that the child also knows the meaning. This is especially important if the word is a homonym. It is a good idea always to use the word in a sentence, so that there is no doubt as to what you mean. A sentence or two for dictation is recommended to give the child further reinforcement using the word in its appropriate sense. Sentences should however be matched for phonic content and fitted to the cumulative programme. Spelling and sound patterns that have not been taught should not be included. Increase the length of the sentences gradually as the child progresses. In this way the child's working memory span can be expanded.

Grammar and punctuation

Grammar is about the correct use of words in language. We generally learn about grammar in its written form through our use of grammar in its oral form (speech), so if we say, "Yous are going to town" instead of "You are going to town", this is likely to be what you will write. Young people with dyslexia are no more likely than anyone else to make errors of this sort though they may misspell words more often. Because we do not connect punctuation directly to oral language, this is an area that young people with dyslexia can find difficult. They often forget to put capital letters in the right places and/or to insert commas and full stops, particularly when concentrating on the content of their writing. Punctuation does have to be taught directly as it does for the majority of children. However, often children with dyslexia do not remember the mechanics of capitalisation and the various elements of punctuation. As with other aspects of language, practice to the point of overlearning is needed till punctuation becomes automatic.

Start with the most common elements of punctuation – capital letters and full stops, and then commas and question marks followed by quotation marks and the less common aspects.

It is best to concentrate only on one aspect at a time when children are writing creatively; e.g. get them to attempt to get all their capital letters in the right place. Children with dyslexia often capitalise letters in the middle of words and there are various reasons for this. Sometimes it is because of difficulty with handwriting the lower case letters, sometimes they cannot remember which way round or which way up the lower case letter should face (b,d, p,q, n,u, m,w for example). It is therefore important that they learn where and when a capital letter is important; at the start of a sentence, for proper nouns, after a full stop or an exclamation mark. We use capital letters for titles, notices and contractions. The finer elements can be taught later once the basics are mastered.

Paragraphing a piece of writing is important and children with dyslexia will require strategies to help them think about how this can best be done. Planning ahead generally helps – using a mind map, simple headings, the hamburger analogy (pg. 105) and other strategies. **See section on Continuous Prose Writing** which follows for suggestions. Young people should think of paragraphs as having a topic sentence followed by supporting sentences and a concluding sentence. This can be illustrated by Red, Amber and Green highlighters for practice – Red for the key idea of the paragraph at the start, Amber or Yellow for the supporting ideas which elaborate the initial sentence and Green for the concluding sentence which summarises what has gone before. The act of highlighting the elements that make up their paragraphs acts as a visual reminder to students of how paragraphs are generally structured.

Handwriting

Though it seems that computers have now taken over the task of handwriting for us, there are still good reasons why handwriting is important, though undoubtedly its importance is significantly less than it was a few decades ago. The teaching of handwriting should accompany the teaching of a phoneme as part of a structured literacy programme.

When teaching a single letter sound or pattern of letters, the child should be encouraged to write the appropriate letter or letters while simultaneously learning the sound. This does not have the same effect if a computer key is pressed! As soon as the child is able to write the correct letter shape, it is important to teach an appropriate cursive style of handwriting. An appropriate style would be one that is very similar to the school's own, but with the necessary joining strokes added if they are not there.

The examples that follow overleaf show lower case letters which include the necessary ligatures to enable the child to join every letter in a word. Capital letters would not join.

Aa Bb Cc Dd Ee Ff Gg Hh Ii Jj Kk Ll Mm Nn Oo Pp Qq Rr Ss Tt Uu Vv Ww Xx Yy Zz or y

Reasons for using a cursive style:

- To encourage a left- right progression

- To eliminate uncertainty over where to start the different letters

- To increase the child's confidence by joining all the lower case letters

- To avoid confusion of the ball and stick letters – e.g. b, d, p and q are less easily confused than b, d, p and q

- To encourage correct placement and sizing of letters: - e.g. splint is better than spliNt

- To obtain an automatic written response when forming handwritten letters which will not have to be changed later

- To encourage the natural flow of sound into shape through the movement of the hand

- Digraphs are written as one unit of sound

- To encourage the writing of irregular words to become an automatic response

- To develop a flowing, reasonably swift style of handwriting and reduce the amount of time taken.

There may be a few problems to begin with in linking the visual image which the children see on notice boards and books to that which they handwrite. This is something that children will overcome through practice and will have to overcome at some stage anyway whether or not a fully cursive style is used. The main advantage is that the uncertainty over where to start and how to proceed are gone – no longer, "Do I join this letter or not?"

Note: All letters should be referred to by their name as well as by their sounds.

For children who are completely lacking in pencil control additional practice can be given by handwriting exercises. There are many resources on the market for this including software packages which can be downloaded, but it is important that the exercises match the style of writing being taught in the classroom. The multisensory practice must be consistent with the technique which is being taught. Before investing money in software packages it is always best to check the appropriateness of the resources. For young people with difficulties, examples which do not match the teaching they have had will only confuse them. When teaching handwriting, a multisensory technique is required.

Procedure for handwriting a phoneme

1. Teacher writes the capital letter on a flipchart or whiteboard and names it, then gives the sound e.g. Writes B, says 'bee', then says the sound - /b/.

2. Teacher prints the lower case letter, shows how approach stroke and carry-on stroke are added, then goes over the whole letter starting from the approach stroke.

3. Teacher writes and names the letter in cursive form, then says the sound.

4. Child traces over letter with finger saying both name and sound.

5. Child takes pen or stylus in dominant hand, rests other hand over it, says the letter name and sound, and repeats the process. This should be done several times until the teacher is satisfied that the child has the 'feel' of the letter and can match letter and sound. The child can also practise writing the letter in the air using a whole arm movement while simultaneously naming the letter and sound. Asking the child to write the letter on the board with eyes shut forces him to concentrate his efforts on the hand and arm movements necessary to produce the letter. This gives additional input and is a useful exercise while at the same time introducing an element of fun.

   In the case of a digraph such as 's', 'h' making the sound /sh/, the same procedure should be adopted, the child saying both letters - 'ess', 'aitch', then /sh/.

From here the child progresses to writing the letter or letters in his jotter, firstly alone, then as part of a word, then in a sentence. A comfortable seating position should always be adopted. The angle of the jotter or notepad will depend on whether she is left or right handed. Though the majority of the world is right-handed and write with their right hand (around 90%), left-handed children should never be forced to write with their right hand. All children should be allowed to establish a dominant hand for themselves. This has often already happened by the time children come to school.

Position for right hander   **Position for left hander**

The use of lined paper is advised if the child has difficulty writing in a straight line. This also helps with the positioning of letters and spacing between lines. Tramline paper is available from suppliers such as Hope Education and is useful for guidance in the early stages of handwriting or where difficulty persists. See **Appendix 2 under Handwriting**. If the child requires to include drawings as part of the written work, then a jotter with one page lined and one page blank will be of use. Alternatively a sheet with heavily marked lines can be placed under the blank page so that the child can see the lines underneath to give guidance.

If the child has a wrong or poor grip of the pencil, a pencil grip may well prove useful. These come in a range of styles and are available also for left-handers. It is best to try these out as not all young people like them or feel that they help. For older children who would be embarrassed by using a grip, but still need to correct their pencil hold, three-sided pencils often prove successful.

Continuous Prose Writing

The writing of continuous prose is a step which follows on from the ability to read, write and spell. As these improve, so should the ability and desire to produce acceptable prose. The writing of prose however involves the interaction of all the skills the child has been learning and a few others, a much more complex skill. For a story to make sense the child's working memory will have to operate at an acceptable level. As working memory is often an area of weakness, then training in working memory skills will give multiple benefits. **See section on Memory** for ideas on how to develop memory and sustain improvements.

The child has to be able to think what he wishes to say, put his words into a sentence and retain for long enough to set them down on paper or other means. This can be a task of considerable difficulty to the child with dyslexia as the sequence of the sentence or indeed the whole sequence of the story can become jumbled as he tries to think of spelling, punctuation, grammatical factors and all the other necessary skills for putting together an acceptable story. For this reason, pressure to produce accurate continuous prose should not be the main priority in the early stages. Even at later stages teaching should be focused on developing the child's creative abilities rather than the scribing skills that can be readily supported by technology if and when necessary.

Assessment of writing for children and young people can be tricky as they are inhibited by an empty page. Sometimes starting from a picture, cartoon or writing frame will help get the process of writing started. The child should be instructed not to worry about spelling or grammar. However some analysis of that too can be informative.

We do not wish to inhibit the flow of words or constrain the creative development of a storyline by constant worry over mechanical sub-skills. If spelling and punctuation do not come automatically, the effort of concentration on composition and content means spelling and punctuation are liable to be forgotten. These can however be improved by encouraging the child to self-correct his work when finished. Train the child to look over his work critically and try to spot any errors.

He can mark his own corrections above the error, and in this way the teacher can see the mistakes that are spotted and those which are not. The teacher can then see how skills of self-correction are developing (or not). If the work is for something important, then a redraft can be done.

However it is important to consider the age of the child as redrafting can be a disincentive to writing, and technology will provide a more motivating option. If a redraft is attempted, do not expect the result to be error free as copying from corrections can be difficult. When working memory skills are weak, the child may not be able to retain the sequence of letters in a word in memory for long enough to transcribe it correctly or it may become jumbled in the process of transcription. If technology is being used there is no need for drafting and redrafting. A hand-drawn plan or mind map however may be desired. There are illustrations of mind maps later in the book.

The value of redrafting however must be seriously considered to avoid children becoming demotivated. Word processors, predictive text, speech to text should be considered. These are not instant alternatives to writing as coaching will be required to ensure the child learns competence but they are likely to provide a good long-term solution especially for the older child who is struggling.

As adults we all depend on technology. The generation now in school have grown up knowing no other world so technology should hold no fear for them, and if they are dyslexic then the computer can provide much of the help they need. They do however need a knowledgeable adult or a sensitive 'study buddy' to keep them on the right track. With the appropriate help and support the need for redrafting work and for rewriting will be eliminated.

Spelling can be greatly improved by the use of the facility to check spelling included in word processors. Young people will then be aware of the words they need to leave alone. A person with dyslexia can often look at a word that is spelled correctly and wonder whether or not it is wrong. The spell-checking facility, through highlighting only the incorrect words and providing likely alternatives and their correct spellings, can itself be responsible for an improvement in spelling.

Structuring writing

The child or young person with dyslexia will often lack any kind of structure for their ideas and it helps if they have a specific skeleton structure that they can follow to give order and sequence to stories and descriptive writing. Children can be given a specific structure that they can follow on all occasions for particular pieces and types of writing. It will help too if they are able to visualise the structure. For example, a piece of descriptive writing might consist of:

1. Introduction of important characters – who are the most important players?
2. Setting for the story – where is it taking place?
3. What happens first (e.g. In the beginning).
4. The main part of the story – the exciting part leading to the climax who does what to whom and why?
5. The solution – how does the story work out, or not?
6. The conclusion – happy, sad, emotional response.

Descriptive Writing

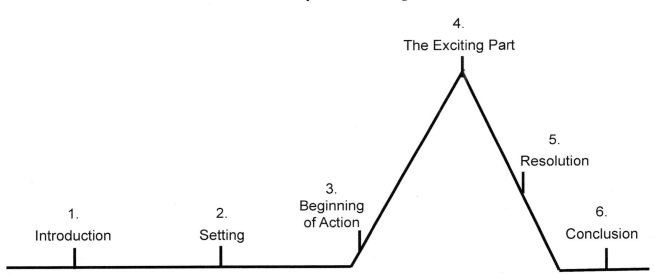

With descriptive writing it is a good idea to introduce the idea of a Beginning, a Middle and an End. To encourage writing ideas in sequence, initial paragraph headings drafted onto sticky notes should bring some order into what otherwise might turn out to be a disjointed piece of work.

For older students, the hamburger analogy can be useful for presenting an argument:

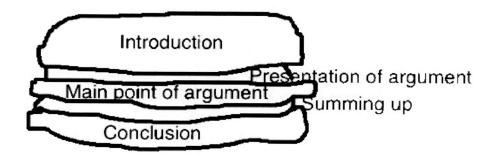

The Hamburger analogy

The top and bottom of the roll or bap represent the Introduction and the Conclusion. The butter is the presentation of the argument/s. The burger is the meaty part in the middle that contains the substance and development of the argument/s. The butter on the other side (the lower part) is the Summing Up of the findings, leading to the lower part of the roll – the Conclusion.

While these plans will help ensure correct sequencing most young people will need encouragement to expand their writing, to build up atmosphere and put in the fine detail that is required to form an interesting story or piece of descriptive writing. This can only be achieved gradually and by discussing with the individual how they can improve their current efforts.

For the child or young person with dyslexia who has severe difficulties or who is unable to produce prose writing in an understandable form, it may be best to allow them to produce their story or description as a series of pictures. Divide up the page into around six sections, like a cartoon strip and only request that the child writes one sentence about each picture. This will be enough to work on if there are considerable numbers of errors. Encourage the production of short sentences initially and build on this.

Cartoon Strip

Writing frames

For children and young people who are reluctant to begin writing, writing frames can help get over the fear that is generated through looking at an empty page. The young person can be presented with an attractive page with a brief outline of what is expected. These frames can be either for use with paper and pencil or for writing on the computer or tablet, but the principle is the same – an attractive task, even for those who have very little literacy and writing skill. The teacher or classroom assistant can create a well-designed frame or select from the range of pre-designed material available from a range of suppliers. The important point is that very little writing is required and the frame facilitates the task. So for example, the child may be being asked to write about their pet. In the frame is a rectangular section for a drawing of the pet. The child can then write the name of the pet or if they are more fluent, write something about the animal. There is then a section entitled, " Where my pet lives" and another "What my pet eats". The final one leaves scope for the learner to develop anything else he wants to say. This is entitled, "More about my pet". The final presentation, no matter the level the child is at, should be quite acceptable and provide a sample of written work that the teacher can use to build upon. There is a sample on the CD.

Mind Maps

Another effective method of planning for writing is to use a mind map. There are several examples of mind maps later in this book. The idea of using a mind map for planning essays and other pieces of writing is that the person can start with a central idea (as those with dyslexia often do) and from there put all their ideas down on paper, computer or tablet. This is likely to resemble the way they are thinking and may be extremely creative but seemingly quite disorganised. When the ideas are all there on the paper, they can then number them and sort them into a sensible order according to the topic they are going to write about. If a digital mind map is used, they can move these ideas about and re-organise them into what they see as a useful outline without the need for rewriting or scribbling changes onto paper. When this is done, they are ready to start writing. With older students this is likely to give them a whole essay outline or framework for their piece of writing. Any sequencing difficulties will be minimised, and the fear that they previously faced of a blank sheet of paper will be gone. Many people (dyslexic and non-dyslexic) also use mind maps to plan talks, study for exams and help with memory problems. Mind maps can be extremely useful for a range of functions and can be paper and pencil or digital.

Video

Recent research has shown film can be a powerful tool to help improve children's reading and writing. Video can be used to develop a range of abilities, such as decoding, inference and analysis, as well as expanding creativity and improving vocabulary. Video is integral to modern children's lives.

From an early age children learn to use remote controls to operate a television and video. The provision of moving images in school provides a link to the world that children experience in the home and in their lives. Film can stimulate creativity through engaging children in developing a plot, describing a scene, making an argument, understanding cultural and societal issues and situations.

For young people with dyslexia who often find writing a chore and a tremendous effort, film can provide stimuli for reading and writing and is likely to provide a bridge for establishing basic skills and from there developing higher order skills of comprehension and inference. The similarities between the process of film making and planning a piece of writing can provide children with a model for story writing – planning a sequence of shots, who and what will be in them, the importance of lighting and colour in setting the scene, consideration of camera angle, movement, building information, ideas, implications, time and distance, making the film, editing and final cut.

All the visual imagery in film has parallels in writing that young people can consider and determine how they can create that imagery for themselves through their writing. Young people need to feel that they can succeed in creating scenes both through the use of a camera and through the power of words. Both can be potent. For this reason, marking of writing has to be done in an empathic way so that learners remain motivated and their engagement with words is not stifled.

Marking

In handwritten work do not mark anything the child is not expected to amend. It is demoralising for a child to see a large number of corrections on his book and to have no opportunity to better this. It is better to put items that the child is expected to rectify in a margin at the side of the page. Even though the margin may have several marks, once corrected the child's own efforts still look reasonable. A code should be devised if there is not already a standard code for the whole school (e.g. Sp. for 'spelling of word to be corrected', C for 'capital letter needed', F.S. for 'full stop required', etc.

This code should be used for the whole class or whole school and should be put on the wall so that all the children can benefit from the system. It is best not to over-correct. If there are too many points to attend to, the child will not remember. It is far better to concentrate on a few points, perhaps only on errors of the same type, or work already covered, and work on other points at a different stage.

Chapter 8

Mathematics and Numeracy

A few children with specific learning difficulties have no associated problems in the mathematical field. However, for the vast majority of those with dyslexia, there is some overlap. This often affects:

- The ability to read, and hence understand, the problems or questions set
- The learning of number bonds involved in addition and subtraction
- The learning of multiplication tables
- The understanding of concepts involving directionality – e.g. time and spatial concepts. Confusion can also arise through having to process different operations in different directions: Starting at the right in addition, subtraction and multiplication, but at the left when dividing.
- Sequencing activities - remembering a sequence such as days in the week, months in the year
- Orientation - getting numbers the right way round and right way up is sometimes an associated problem: 5 for 2, 6 for 9, etc.
- Spatial awareness and ability to correctly position figures on a page and hence get the numbers in the right column, etc.
- Visual discrimination resulting in confusion of signs such as: + , ÷ , x , < >, etc.
- Holding information in memory for long enough to do a calculation, mental arithmetic.

This book does not attempt to cover the topic of dyscalculia nor does it try to draw a boundary between where difficulties with numeracy/mathematics and dyscalculia lie. There is no doubt a group of students for whom both dyslexia and dyscalculia overlap. The focus here is on dyslexia and how difficulties due to dyslexia might affect students in their numeracy and mathematics and considers what teachers can do to help learners overcome or circumvent difficulties.

Maths Anxiety

Maths anxiety is the feeling of tension that interferes with the manipulation of numbers and tackling of mathematical problems in day-to-day situations. It is a negative emotional reaction which can affect children in school when faced with a mathematical or numeric problem. Maths anxiety often co-occurs with dyslexia and dyscalculia though it should not be confused with dyscalculia. One major effect of maths anxiety is its impact on working memory. Maths anxiety can be exacerbated by parental anxiety over maths. One way of helping students who are troubled by anxiety is to allow them to discuss their fears in a safe situation.

It could be that there are a number of students who are affected and can help one another. Another way of increasing children's confidence in their abilities is to move them on at a steady pace, but always ensuring they are able to cope. Ensure that children are not asked to do something they have not been taught and understood.

Because the majority of maths books require a reasonable level of competence in reading even at the early stages, teachers need to be aware that children with dyslexia will need additional support to help them cope. Worksheets with simple vocabulary will help. Check that the child knows the words in the differentiated version. Pairing the child with a good reader can be advantageous provided the good reader in not also doing all the work. We must ensure at all costs that the learner with dyslexia is not held back from advancing knowledge of mathematical concepts purely because he has poor reading ability.

To establish the main difficulties in mathematical skills, some form of assessment is necessary. Some information may already be available if a dyslexia assessment has been done, but more finely tuned evidence will be helpful. Number screening will give some information and this can be further broken down by assessment of particular areas of numeracy or maths. Criterion referenced assessment should also help determine precise areas of need and difficulties highlighted can be further investigated to discover any underlying reasons for the mathematical difficulties.

Numeracy problems, like language and literacy problems, lie in putting together the little skills necessary to achieve overall competence. Directional confusion, poor sequencing, working memory weaknesses, poor spatial awareness, visual perceptual difficulties and weak literacy skills are all just as important here as they are in language work, with the added complication that computation does not always operate in a left-right progression. There is also the possibility that when adding for example, one teacher may start from the top and another from the bottom. For the child with poor directional sense, this can be very confusing. Teachers should be aware of this and if there is not already a specific policy on this, should insist that a whole school shares the same policy.

The principles of multisensory teaching that apply to language work also apply to the mathematical field. Progress must be carefully monitored at each stage, checking that a particular concept has been thoroughly mastered before moving on to the next step. A checklist is often the simplest way of doing this provided there is space for additional notes to keep track of the exact nature of any difficulties.

An example is given below of a checklist that is typical of those used to ensure there is detailed tracking of needs and progress towards meeting those needs and filling any gaps in knowledge and/or understanding. Schools can readily make their own lists of skills bearing in mind that the attainment targets will need to be broken down sufficiently to ensure that they will accurately describe the skills and needs of each child individually and reflect the difficulties which they are experiencing.

For example, columns can be used to tick when a child has been taught a specific item, whether they can still do it a week later, a month later, etc. and when the teacher is satisfied the child can use the skill consistently.

Addition Checklist			
	Sound Knowledge	Erratic	Specific errors
One to one correspondence of numbers to 10	☐	☐	
Adds numbers within 5 using concrete materials	☐	☐	
Adds numbers within 10 using concrete materials	☐	☐	
Adds numbers within 5 without concrete materials	☐	☐	
Adds numbers within 10 without concrete materials	☐	☐	
Adds numbers within	☐	☐	

For some children with specific learning difficulties, the very language and symbolic nature of mathematical material is in itself a major problem. For these children it is necessary to clarify the terms we use. Terms such as 'multiply', 'divide', 'subtraction' and similar terms may in themselves pose problems that can prevent the child from progressing in simple arithmetic skills. When the initial concepts are understood, the symbols and terms we wish the child to know can be put onto cards so they can become familiar with them and practise them till they become automatic.

The examples which follow show cards for 'addition' and 'greater than', but these can be made up for any of the numeric and mathematical language terms we wish the child to master. These should be tailored to the individual child's needs at any one time. They should be built up gradually as the child requires – perhaps, 'add' and 'and' may be sufficient for the child initially, later supplementing this with 'find the sum of', 'increase by', etc.

Daily practice of the cards by looking at the front, recalling what is written on the back and checking that they have remembered the various items correctly, can be carried out by the child either individually or with a partner. In the same way, 'find the sum of' could be printed on the front of the card and alternatives written on the back alongside the symbol '+', if this would be more useful for the child.

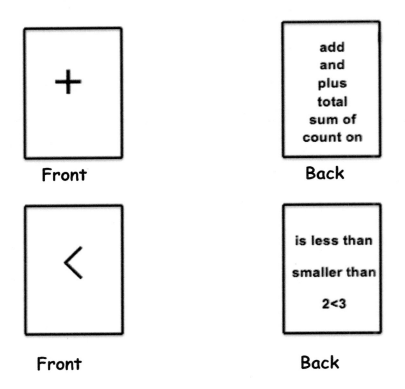

Front · Back

Front · Back

Because of sequencing difficulties, even a child who has mastered his number bonds may still arrive at the wrong answer.

In this addition, the child knows his number bonds and is saying, "Nine and six are fifteen", but then writes down the one instead of the five, and carries the five instead of one.

Even more complex sequencing errors are often found. It is well worthwhile asking children how they arrived at an answer before assuming they simply can't do it or are weak in number bonds. One simple sequencing error can completely knock out the whole calculation. When dealing with a problem of this nature it may be a considerable help to children if they are allowed to use a jotter with boxes. Encouraging the child to head columns with 'Hundreds', 'Tens', 'Units' (H,T,U) may also help. The child must actively consider that if he has fifteen, he has one ten and five units. The use of concrete material (manipulatives) beyond the time when we would expect the child to dispense with these will provide an additional support.

Often though the child has understood the concepts and needs multisensory practice in the sequence of numbers in order that he may write them correctly. If children practise saying, "Fifteen: one ten and five units" or "One ten and five singles", as they write the numbers, they will learn to think which number comes first. When doing calculations then, if the children first mark the columns with the appropriate headings, the sequence of the numbers should prove easier.

Manipulatives

The term 'manipulatives' applies to all the various pieces of kit that can be helpful in a practical way when children and young people are learning to use numbers – Dienes apparatus, Cuisenaire rods, Multilink cubes, counters and any other pieces of equipment that might be used. Using manipulatives in a multi-sensory way to reinforce actions is helpful. Children should say what the piece of equipment is doing for them as they illustrate the calculation or counting exercise, and then write down in numeric language the calculation they have just done.

Children should not think that one manipulative is used for one specific task never to be seen again because that one task has been mastered. It is important to ensure that children see the value in retaining the use of manipulatives as a multisensory learning device rather than just a crutch to be used for a short time that is easily dispensed with. Manipulatives have a multitude of uses, and it is likely that learners with dyslexia will require to use these materials as supports beyond the time when others have dispensed with them. It is important to ensure understanding of concepts and that the young person is not delayed in progression due to a lack of practical resources or due to reading difficulties.

For difficulties with number bonds and tables, many of the same principles apply as have been discussed before. The first step as always is to ensure that the child has a sound understanding of the concepts involved and has had adequate practice using concrete materials and aids, e.g. by sorting activities, one-to-one correspondence, grouping in tens, etc. He must also have a sound knowledge of the symbols involved and be encouraged to look at these carefully to ensure he fully understands the nature of the task.

For the child who does not yet understand the concept of number and associating symbols with a particular number of items (for example, a child who cannot recognise that **O O O** represents three dots and the symbol '3') sets of wooden or plastic numbers should be used to give the child multisensory practice and to help understanding.

Wooden numbers that have the number of dots etched out on the back of each number are particularly useful. The child can actually feel the number shape and count at the same time.

The technique for practising writing the numbers can be practised similarly to that of the graphemes:

1. Teacher writes the number on the board and names it, e.g. writes 3 – says, "Three", and then draws three dots, saying, "One, two, three", as he does so.

2. Child traces over the number and dots, counting out exactly as the teacher has done.

3. Child takes a felt pen, or a finger of their dominant hand, rests other hand on top and repeats the process several times, until the teacher is happy that the child is confident.

4. Child then proceeds to writing the number in his jotter in the usual way accompanied by three dots.

Place Value

There is a considerable amount of structured concrete material available from educational suppliers to help in understanding place value. It is important for all children to get practice in using this type of material, but it is even more important for children with specific learning difficulties as their difficulties in setting down their work and sense of directionality and sequencing can often be mistaken for lack of understanding. For children who have difficulties in working with numbers in columns, partitioning may be their preferred method of solving a problem. For example, when adding 37 and 48, adding 30 to 40, then adding 7 to 8, and then adding together 70 and 15 to give 85 may be as logical as adding the units first and then carrying the ten. With concrete material children will be able to understand that there is more than one way to tackle mathematical calculations.

It is important first and foremost that they understand the concepts. Difficulty with memory may mean that even when the concepts are understood, children still get the wrong answer. When attempting to change children from the use of a partitioning method to working in columns, then a boxed jotter where they can mark the columns as hundreds, tens, units etc may help. However it is important to understand HOW a child gets an answer. Understanding how they have worked out their answer (right or wrong) will help us establish what is understood and what is not, and if there is understanding of the main concepts we are trying to establish, the memory difficulties can be tackled.

When it has been established that children understand a concept, any fact we wish memorised can be put on cards in the way described previously, as remembering may often be a problem for number bonds, multiplication tables, etc.

Put the problem on one side and the answer on the other so that children can practise on their own and self-correct if necessary, the principle again being to add cards in a structured cumulative way.

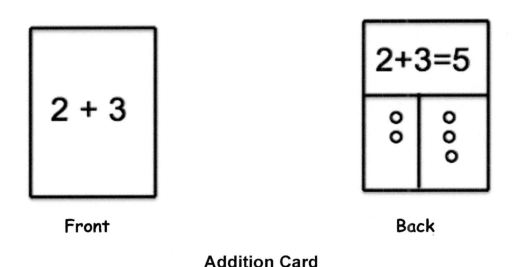

Front   Back

Addition Card

The number of cards which should be added each day should follow the principle of giving children success as an aid to motivation – success with some challenge! If children see themselves progressing, even if it is only by one number bond or table fact each day, then this is probably more than they have managed previously and can act as encouragement. If pushed too hard and expected to learn too many facts children will soon become exasperated and give up trying, exacerbating the problem. Previously learned facts should be quickly 'run-through' each day. If children practise in pairs, it is a good idea to get them to say out the whole bond, "3+2=5", rather than just the answer. This gives reinforcement of the whole bond. Children should also be given an opportunity to write these out in some way while saying them, giving true, multisensory learning. This should not however become laboured. For extra practice, with children in a circle, teacher throws a beanbag and says a number bond (or other fact we want the children to memorise) and each child gives a quick-fire response. Only do this once the children have a reasonably good grasp of the points.

If the child cannot be partnered with another who is having difficulties with the number bonds or other area, then again parents may be a useful resource. To avoid this taking excessive time at home, children should only have a few bonds, facts or formulae to practise by writing out each night. This will of course include the bond or bonds added that day, and a few others. The bonds not written, should be quickly 'run through' orally. Parents can also be encouraged to play number games with the children at home. Again we have to be careful that the children know the facts involved in the game, and that the games approach is only used as reinforcement. If the child is unable to produce the answers readily he will soon become demotivated no matter what the approach.

Use of Technology

Audacity is free open source digital audio recording and editing software that can be used on almost any computer. As such it is a useful tool for recording for use in the classroom. Recording of the number bonds and multiplication tables is a useful method of establishing facts that can be made self-correcting by appropriate use of the software, the child being able to work on her own with a minimum of instruction and supervision from the teacher. For example, if a group of children are having problems with a particular multiplication table, then they can work together. The recording made by the teacher must proceed at a pace to suit the children. First the teacher records the whole table, saying each fact slowly and precisely. Then the teacher records the table, hesitating for a pause before each answer to give the child a chance to 'beat the teacher'. Then the table is presented in random order, again with the teacher hesitating before giving the answer, allowing sufficient time for the child to think of the answer first.

A further step is then added where the child is asked to write down the fact along with the answer, the teacher providing the answers on a separate sheet for the child to correct later. This ensures that the child does not cheat and wait for the teacher's answer, although it should be emphasised to her that as she is not being closely supervised the only person she can effectively 'cheat' is herself. It is best to record each table separately so the recording is a short length and the child can easily find the point in the table she wants to be at. When the child has practised all the individual tables and can happily answer most of each table, she can go on to a recording which contains random examples from the different tables, presented in different ways.

Other software too can be given as an incentive to learning for the child who 'almost knows' his facts or bonds. Several programs are available which present material in an attractive way. For practice of some of the basic skills, programs such as Numbershark and Dynamo Maths can give much needed overlearning to give confidence without boredom. There are many other programs that will help the learner progress in numeric and mathematical skills. These are not however a substitute for sound multisensory teaching but they can extend and enhance existing good practice.

For children with severe difficulties or children who simply do not have the time to spend on these strategies without falling further behind, the use of a number square, calculator or spread sheet should be encouraged.

> The argument that if the child uses a calculator she will never learn the facts is irrelevant. Even if the child has to rely on a prop of this nature for the rest of her life, she should not be deterred from progressing to the next stage in understanding mathematical concepts just because she is unable to rote learn a sequence of bonds or facts.

Many children with specific learning difficulties have difficulty in distinguishing their left from their right. For the 90% of children who are right-handed the mnemonic, "You write with your right hand" might work.

Telling the Time

Much practice however is often necessary with the terms 'left', 'right', 'up', 'down', 'before', 'after', 'to', 'past', etc. and children can be asked frequently to describe relative positions. A clearly structured sequence of exercises showing progression to enable the child to practise regularly may help a child who is experiencing difficulties with orientation. This will probably start simply with exercises such as, "Point to your left ear" and progress through, "Touch your right knee with your left hand", and finally hope to be able to complete tasks such as "Point to my left ear with your right hand". 'O'Grady-type' games can be used as a fun way of reinforcing orientation skills , e.g. with children standing in a safe space, teacher says, "O'Grady says touch your right knee."

"Touch your left shoulder with your right hand," etc. If the teacher says the sentence without putting "O'Grady says ....." in front, and the child does the action, then the child has to sit down and is out of the game. The last child standing is the winner. A programme of activities that might help with this is given in the **section on Physical Education** that follows.

Once it has been established that the child understands the concepts of 'to' and 'past', and can tell 'left' from 'right', telling the time can be introduced in the usual order. Introduce multisensory techniques as much as possible. The use of a geared clock is recommended, so that the child can sense the idea of the passage of time while they can at the same time practise saying the time aloud. The idea of self-corrective practice cards described earlier is once again useful in this area to give regular reinforcement without constant teacher supervision. The learner will require to consider digital time as well, but it is worthwhile at the start to ensure the student has a sense of the passage of time that he will get from an analogue clock with hands. This seems less realistic using a digital clock or watch, even though it may be easier to understand.

Clock Card

Games (see Appendix 2) might also bring added incentive and motivation to what can otherwise become very tedious but nonetheless necessary reinforcement. Games such as Time Dominoes and Time Snap where learners match the digital with the analogue times can reinforce both 12 and 24-hour clocks and give comparisons of analogue and digital times. With adequate initial teaching and teacher supervision, these can be both helpful and effective.

If older children are still having difficulties it is appropriate to look at approaches to circumvent the problem areas while not giving up on the possibility of mastering time at a later stage. If children and young people require to know the time to catch buses to school and to be at certain places on time they can use a digital timepiece (watch and/or mobile phone if they can cope with this, rather than persist in trying to learn analogue time when this has already exhausted them. It must of course be established that the young person understands the relationship between times: that they know that 'ten to eleven' and '10:50' are the same; also that if it is 'twelve minutes past ten', and they have to be at the train station for 'quarter past ten', then they have no time to spare.

Although difficulties relating to dyslexia often affect children's progress in the field of mathematics they should not be an insuperable obstacle and need not prevent progress. What we must guard against is holding the child back for too long because she has not mastered a certain task. It is far better to find a strategy to circumvent the problem in order that the child can continue to progress with her group rather than impede progress unnecessarily.

There may be arguments about whether a learner has dyscalculia or difficulties with mathematics, and whether these difficulties are specific or not. As with dyslexia, this is dependent on how we define the difficulties – in this case how we define 'dyscalculia'. For the purposes of this book however, no matter whether the difficulties are due to dyslexia or dyscalculia as a separate entity, these difficulties need to be tackled and learners supported to improve their skills.

Chapter 9

Health and Wellbeing

Within the curriculum areas covered under the Health and Wellbeing area, it is worth giving specific regard to how Physical Education and movement can help pupils with dyslexia and some of the specific difficulties they may have. This of course might also be reflected in the Expressive Arts where dance and movement can prove useful ways of motivating and strengthening skills.

Mental Health

With appropriate help and support in school and at home, dyslexia should not in itself cause mental health problems. However when dyslexia remains unrecognised it can result in low self-esteem and a lack of motivation. This can be a source of concern and can exacerbate the individual's learning difficulties. Over time if children are met with negative feedback they can 'opt out' and fall into a state of learned helplessness. Dyslexia is inextricably a part of the individual and inevitably affects how children feel about themselves as they grow up. The emotional impact that dyslexia has on the individual must always be considered so that the child develops understanding of what it is to be dyslexic and how to overcome the feelings of negativity that sometimes seem overwhelming. It is important then for teachers to consider the strengths that children bring to tasks, stress what they are good at, and ensure that that the weak areas of functioning are explained and given appropriate support.

Physical Education and Movement

Not all children and young people with specific learning difficulties present problems in the area of physical education, but some do present problems of clumsiness and lack motor control. Sometimes overlapping difficulties are severe enough to be considered as developmental co-ordination disorder (DCD) or dyspraxia. If difficulties are severe, then an occupational therapist (OT) can offer exercises and practical help that parents and teachers can support. For those with more minor difficulties, teachers can offer a structured exercise programme that is likely to be of benefit to a number of children. Though there is not a lot of research evidence for intensive physical therapy improving reading and writing as some would have us believe, it is likely that a programme of physical exercises will have a beneficial effect on health generally and if specifically targeted, can help confidence and give other 'knock-on' benefits. At worst a physical programme will increase the flow of oxygen through the body, including the brain, and help attention and concentration through increased alertness. At best it will not only give these benefits but also may improve co-ordination, handwriting and have accompanying effects on learning. It is therefore worth considering this area separately.

Children with dyslexia may have visual sequencing and/or auditory sequencing problems that will benefit from a carefully organised programme in a suitable space. We have to be careful that our intervention does not interfere excessively with the normal development of a child who is happy and enjoys their physical education lessons.

If the child has gross motor problems, the teacher has to be particularly sensitive as the child will very easily become discouraged by lack of ability and may not wish to take part. Alternatively they may present with behaviour problems as an avoidance tactic. If dealt with empathetically however a child with dyslexia, and indeed all children, can gain considerably from a carefully planned physical programme.

Research into the role of regular physical exercise in helping children's development overall has been positive. In an already packed curriculum, however, teachers find it difficult to offer carefully structured programmes designed to promote effective learning on a daily basis. Activities should be devised, as with the rest of the teaching, as part of a carefully planned and administered multisensory programme. One or two periods of physical education per week may not be enough to help the child with specific difficulties. On the contrary these sessions may only serve to reinforce the feelings of failure the child is already experiencing in their peer group. Self-esteem and confidence can consequently be destroyed. Stage by stage progression of a prescriptive type of approach is advised until self-confidence is sufficient for the child to participate with the rest of the class without fear of ridicule.

The key to any intervention is to start whenever concerns are apparent and progress in small steps that are manageable for the child. The evidence is that early intervention is likely to prevent more serious difficulties later, and that it is best to start with children at an early stage – probably nursery – and progress very gradually and in a fun way, ensuring the child enjoys the activities and is making steady progress.

The following programme, based on original work by the late Professor Bryant J Cratty, is an illustration of how physical exercise can help confusion over right and left, a confusion which affects quite a few people with dyslexia, not just children. The programme can be carried out in a classroom, but care has to be taken to move children away from obstacles that could get in the way. When the teacher says, "Rest", the children return to a relaxed standing position. The time taken for Rest is only a few seconds as the activities should be quite fast-paced. Overall plan on spending around five minutes a day on the activities. With older children a small group of children can be formed and work with a classroom assistant. The activities are best done with a small group.

Stage 1: Ensuring knowledge of left and right in relation to self

With children standing,

1. Hold up both arms. Put them down again. Rest (Do this a few times to ensure children are fully awake and aware.)

2. Raise your left arm. Put it down. Rest. Raise your right arm. Put it down. Rest. Ensure at this point that all children know which is right and which is left.

3. Raise your left arm and your right foot. Rest. Raise your left arm and your left foot. Rest.

Activities that continue these actions and mix up the possible combinations should be completed for at least a week with young children. For older children, the activities would be paced according to how well they cope. Don't move on until the children are all coping well with a stage.

Stage 2: Ensuring knowledge of left and right in relation to external factors

Again with children standing,

1. Quickly review previous moves. Rest. Point to the right-hand wall of the classroom.
2. Point to the left-hand wall of the classroom with your right hand. Rest.
3. Point to the right-hand wall of the classroom with your right hand. Rest.
4. Point to the left-hand wall of the classroom with your left hand. Rest.

Again mix up the possible combinations and carry on the activities, interspersed with previous stage for at least a week.

Stage 3: Ensuring two factor knowledge of left and right

Again with children standing,

1. Quickly review previous moves. Rest. Touch your right knee. Rest. Touch your left knee. Rest.

2. Touch your left ankle with your right hand. Rest. Touch your right elbow with your left hand. Rest.

Mix up the possible combinations as before.

Stage 4: Ensuring left and right in relation to movement

With children standing,

1. Review previous moves. Then select one child at a time for activity.

2. With two chairs. Child walks slowly in figure of eight. Stop at different points. What side is the chair on? Now what side is it on? If child makes a mistake, simply say, "It's on your left this time" or whatever is appropriate.

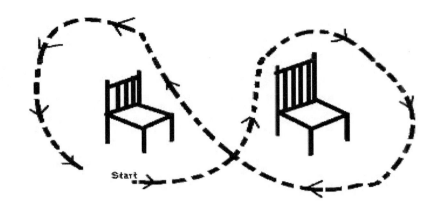

Stage 5: Ensuring knowledge of left and right in relation to others

Children stand and work in pairs. If there is an odd one out, that person works with the teacher.

1. Review selection of previous moves. Then children face one another.
2. Touch your left elbow. Now touch your partner's left elbow.
3. Touch your right ear. Now touch your partner's right ear. Touch your partner's left ear.
4. Touch your partner's right hand.

Mix up possible combinations, but keep fingers away from eyes, especially if there is poor co-ordination.

Stage 6: Ensuring knowledge of left and right in relation to other people

With children standing,

1. Review previous moves. Then select one child at a time for activity.
2. Position a chair or similar object in the middle of the group.
3. Ask, "Is the chair on my left?", "Is the chair on my right?"
4. Select children then to move to beside the chair one at a time. "Is the chair on Jack's left?" Is the chair on Anna's right?" etc ensuring there is some movement of both the chair and the children.

Again mix up the possible combinations of positions and answers.

Stage 7: Ensuring knowledge of left and right in relation to two factors and others

Children stand and work in pairs. If there is an odd one out, that person works with the teacher.

1. Review selection of previous moves. Then children face one another.
2. Touch your left elbow. Now touch your partner's left elbow. Now touch your partner's left elbow with your right hand. Now touch your partner's left elbow with your left hand.
3. Touch your right ear. Now touch your partner's right ear with your left hand. Touch your partner's left ear with your right hand.
4. Touch your partner's right hand with your left hand.

Mix up possible combinations, but keep fingers away from eyes.

Stage 8: Ensuring left and right in relation to movement and others

With children standing,

1. Review previous moves. Then select one child at a time for activity.
2. Teacher dribbles a ball, throws a beanbag or similar. Am I dribbling the ball to left or right? Face different directions starting with back to children then moving in different directions.
3. Select a child to dribble the ball, throw the beanbag. "Is Jack dribbling the ball to left or right?", "Has Anna thrown the beanbag to left or right?"

Changing directions frequently, ensure a mix or different positions and movements.
Observe any children who struggle with the activities and take time intermittently throughout the day to reinforce what has been practised.

For example, as you are looking at the child's work, say quietly, "What side of the desk is your pencil on?", Which hand is my ring on?" etc.

Though this is not strictly speaking a physical education programme, it uses the sense of movement to promote awareness of directionality and how this can change depending on positioning. It also gives children a sense of laterality in relation to themselves and others.

Other structured programmes can be devised to tackle specific areas and it is worthwhile integrating physical movement with a variety of learning tasks. This adds a kinaesthetic element to learning making an integrated multisensory experience for the children. The act of moving serves to keep children alert and promotes active learning.

The notion too of giving children 'brain breaks' where they do activities (e.g. throw a bean bag, follow a series of movements, jump etc) can be integrated with spelling or memory activities (e.g. count up in twos, tens, count backwards, say the alphabet, etc.) so that children make learning experiences more interesting and memorable. Action songs to help remember tables, poems, rhymes and so on make for fun and learning in the classroom.

> Brain breaks can take anything from a couple of minutes to around twenty minutes but should result in the children refocusing while at the same time moving to a purposeful activity.

This is important for all children but for those with a limited attention span, it gives an added dimension in refocusing that is likely to work better than a reprimand.

Mindfulness activities too can be integrated into the classroom, helping children to relax and be aware of their own position in space and how they can activate their brains. Relaxation too is important and with mindfulness. The focus is not only on attention but also on relieving the tension and stress that very often affects those with dyslexia and other specific needs. Programmes are available, for example, to train children to be mindful of listening and other key areas that will make a difference to children's confidence and abilities. The benefit of such a programme is that it can be done with a whole class, and everyone will benefit though some will undoubtedly benefit more than others.

Chapter 10

Foreign Language Learning

Because those with dyslexia have literacy difficulties in learning their own language, it is likely they will also have difficulties is learning another language. However it should not be assumed that this would necessarily be the case. With an appropriate approach difficulties can be minimised and productive learning can occur. Difficulties due to dyslexia that are likely to overlap into foreign language learning are:

- Weakness in phonological processing
- Poor short-term and working memory
- Poor auditory discrimination
- Confusion over syntax
- Faulty auditory sequencing

Visual factors can also affect visual perceptual aspects of language learning causing some confusion over words that appear similar. Teachers should be aware of the areas which dyslexia may affect so these can be taken into account and specific steps taken to maximise learning.

However, it is recommended that every child and young person be given the opportunity to participate in language learning along with their peers as this may well be important for their future life and career. There are many reasons why foreign language learning may be worthwhile, the most important of these being:

- To open up access to culture of another country which may be later required for business or recreational reasons
- To foster identity with those from another country where English is not the main language
- To give experience of aspects of learning another language which will facilitate later learning of any language required due to relocation
- To improve participation and motivation through working alongside peer group
- To help enhance understanding of home language
- To improve cognitive learning
- To help concentration
- To facilitate visits abroad
- To generate confidence if short-term objectives are attainable.

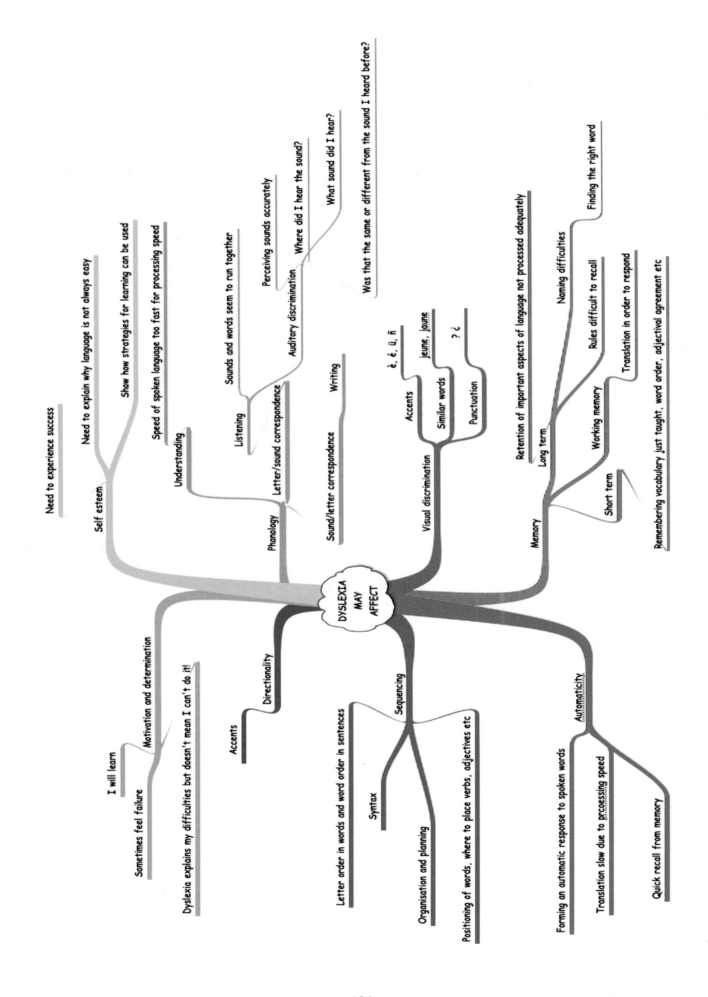

Need to experience success

Self esteem

Need to explain why language is not always easy

Show how strategies for learning can be used

Speed of spoken language too fast for processing speed

Understanding

Listening

Sounds and words seem to run together

Perceiving sounds accurately

Auditory discrimination

Where did I hear the sound?

What sound did I hear?

Was that the same or different from the sound I heard before?

Phonology

Letter/sound correspondence

Writing

Sound/letter correspondence

Visual discrimination

Accents è, é, ü, ñ

Similar words jeune, jaune

Punctuation ? ¿

Retention of important aspects of language not processed adequately

Naming difficulties

Finding the right word

Memory

Long term

Rules difficult to recall

Working memory

Translation in order to respond

Short term

Remembering vocabulary just taught, word order, adjectival agreement etc

DYSLEXIA MAY AFFECT

I will learn

Motivation and determination

Sometimes feel failure

Dyslexia explains my difficulties but doesn't mean I can't do it!

Accents

Directionality

Letter order in words and word order in sentences

Sequencing

Syntax

Organisation and planning

Positioning of words, where to place verbs, adjectives etc

Automaticity

Forming an automatic response to spoken words

Translation slow due to processing speed

Quick recall from memory

Having established that language learning can prove worthwhile for students with dyslexia, there is also a belief that due to the phonological difficulties that learners with dyslexia have, they will benefit more from learning a transparent language (one where the relationship between letters and the sounds they make are constant) – for example, i and e together in German say /ē/ whereas in English (an opaque language) they do not. Consider, for example, words such as 'grief', 'friend', 'conscience' which all contain i and e together. The English language may only have 26 letters, but it has somewhere in the region of 44 sounds. French too has over 38 sounds whereas German and Spanish have around 30 sounds. Transparency of language however is not the only consideration.

While it is true that there are sounds with spellings that are easily confusable in opaque languages, there are other factors that should be considered when determining which language a student with dyslexia would benefit from. Some of these factors are considered above. However we also need to consider other aspects of specific languages before we conclude that a transparent language will be best.

Languages such as Spanish, French or German have gender to consider. Whereas the definite article 'the' in English only has one form, in German there are three gender factors to consider. It can be 'der', 'die' or 'das', and then we must also consider case, so instead of the word 'the' being only 'der', 'die' or 'das', it might be 'den' or 'dem'. Factors relating to case are not the only other consideration. In German too, word order is a factor with verbs being split in certain circumstances.

Adjectival agreement too can be confusing. In English, the adjective will generally precede the noun – 'the big dog', not 'the dog big'. In French however there are specific considerations in placing adjectives – 'une belle maison' (a beautiful house) but 'un chien noir' (a black dog, not a dog black which is what the word order would suggest to an English speaker).

For an individual with dyslexia who has short term or working memory problems as well as sequencing difficulties, remembering all the rules of a language can be just as problematic as understanding the sound system.

Accents used in language may confuse, but on the other hand, they may also simplify, as generally the accent will help determine exactly how the letter is pronounced in sound. Motivation is a strong factor to consider when considering which language to learn – if indeed there is a choice. If a learner is likely to visit or has visited the country then there are clear reasons why a particular language may be the language of choice.

Teaching programmes for learners with dyslexia require material to be presented in a structured and multisensory way with small amounts of information at a time. It is helpful too if class and group numbers can be kept small so that teaching programmes and progress can be closely monitored. Frequent review and repetition will help - vocabulary and common phrases will require considerable overlearning to ensure retention. It is for the teacher to consider how this can be done without boredom, but lots of different approaches and strategies will be useful in presenting the new language in a way that will be acceptable to the learner with dyslexia while at the same time providing a solid base for the student to build on.

Visual aspects can cause confusion – for example accents and words that are visually similar such as 'caballo' (horse) and 'cabello' (hair) in Spanish. The directionality of accents can prove problematic for children who have previously found b/d/p/q confusing. Accents such as é and è, ü and ñ can prove visually confusing. Learners must learn to take context into consideration so they are able to deduce meaning, and information must be presented at a slower speed so that those with dyslexia and other processing difficulties can keep up.

It used to be thought that if students have dyslexia, and have problems with reading, writing and spelling, they should focus only on speaking and listening. They should not have to read, write and spell in a foreign language. There are several reasons why this philosophy does not stand up to scrutiny. Research evidence conducted internationally over a number of years tells us that cutting out channels of learning has a negative impact on learning and instead of promoting learning as we would hope, it does in fact restrict learning considerably.

The level of difficulty a child has in learning their home language may be indicative of how easy or difficult that young person will find learning another language. However this is certainly not the only indicator and it is certainly not prescriptive. Motivation, attitude, awareness of learning styles, self-esteem and determination are all factors which are crucial to the learning process. If young people believe in themselves, this can make the difference between success and failure, so every encouragement should be given to fully participate in all activities.

Multisensory teaching of language, as we have seen, requires the learner to see, hear, speak, write, type, trace or use other kinaesthetic and tactile methods of reinforcing the points. Taking away channels of learning will not be helpful for learning. The senses of taste and smell are more difficult channels to promote, but can still be useful when dealing with topics such as food and drink if learners are encouraged to taste and smell the various samples while naming them and writing or typing out the labels. Discussion and vocabulary promotion can then be encouraged.

If learning and teaching are taken from a multisensory perspective and the child maintains motivation, then it is likely that learning will occur. If the reading and writing aspects prove to be problematic then consideration should be given to whether or not it is appropriate to assess reading and writing. Negative feedback may be discouraging. However the reading and writing elements should not be eliminated as they help provide the multisensory aspects learners need.

Because of phonological difficulties with language generally, there may be problems in picking up the new phonology of a different language. Auditory discrimination can be problematic, so great care needs to be taken to ensure the learner can detect the different sounds of the new language. This is a matter of perception rather than hearing. For example, we may wish to establish if they can detect the difference between /é/ and /è/ in French?

Firstly, the sounds may be problematic so we need to establish if this is the case, and then train listening skills in the language – so, start by finding out if they can hear the sounds – "Where in the word 'église' do you hear the /é/ sound, where do you hear the /é/ in entrée, where do you hear it in élite, émail, café, été, célib?"

Student must say 'beginning', 'middle' or 'end' or a combination as appropriate just as for English language auditory discrimination assessment and training. See section on **Auditory Discrimination**.

"Where in the word 'père' do you hear the /è/ sound, where in 'mère'?" Then combine – "What sound do you hear at the end of the word 'café', in the middle of 'père', at the end of 'thé', at the beginning of 'être', etc.?" It is the sound the student is looking out for here, not the spelling. However, if they can't discriminate between the sounds they are hearing, then spelling will be very difficult. Training in listening for sounds and identifying them correctly will help not just in identifying the words, but also in spelling them correctly.

Once it is established that the learner can discriminate successfully between similar sounds, then it is not necessary to continue checking every sound. If there are difficulties here, training in listening for specific sounds and identifying when they have been heard will be beneficial.

However phonology, being aware of, and gaining an understanding of the sound system of the language, is only one aspect to be taken into account when deciding on a language if there is a choice. All languages have some complexities that mean they differ from the children's home language in some aspects which will require to be mastered if the children are to become competent language learners, speakers and hopefully in time also readers and perhaps writers.

Some considerations in selecting a language when there is choice.

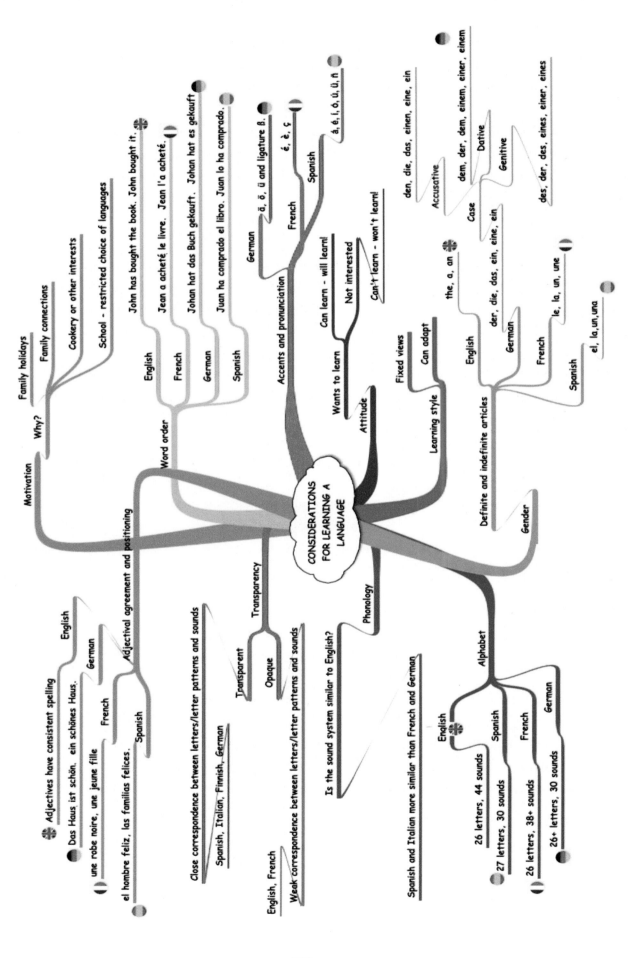

As has been seen, dyslexia can affect a wide range of factors in learning a foreign language just as it has done in a learner's first language. These factors have been previously outlined. Those with dyslexia may have only a few of these pointers, but teachers need to be aware of how dyslexia may impact learning and consider how barriers can be overcome.

Teaching should be multisensory and structured in a way that encourages participation. If something has not been taught then we should not expect our learner to know it. If learning and teaching are taken from a multisensory perspective and the child maintains motivation, then it is likely that learning will occur. Even if we decide that the reading and writing elements of language learning shouldn't be assessed due to the problems learners are having, we should still ensure that these elements are not excluded. The principles for teaching another language are very similar to teaching of home language even though children with dyslexia generally learn to speak their own language before they start school. These principles are summarised below.

Dyslexia: principles for language learning.

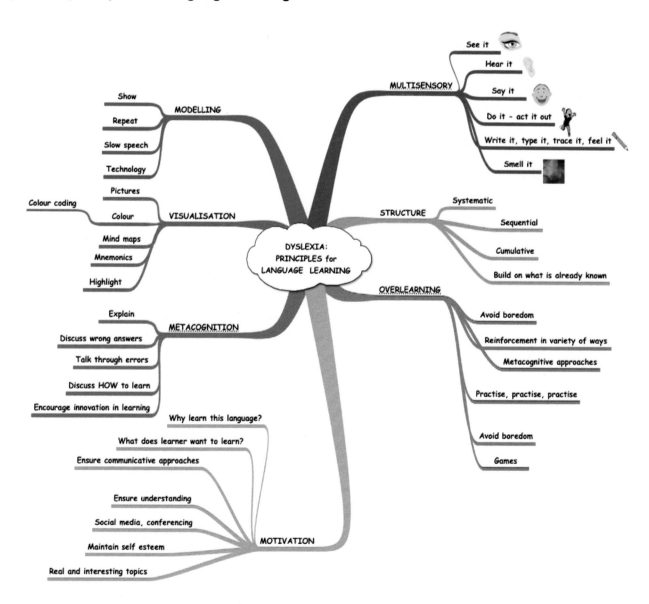

In addition to seeing, hearing, speaking out, writing, typing drawing and acting out, students should be taught to visualise. This can be done in different ways, but should be actively taught rather than expect the learner to pick up the technique. For example, for a learner struggling to distinguish between the German schön (beautiful) and schon (already), they might visualise a beautiful cake adorned with roses. The important point is roundness of the cake and the roundness of the umlauted 'ö' in the cake. They must get a clear picture, so the teacher should discuss and check that the student can visualise – What can you see on the **beautiful** cake?" "What letter is inside the cake?" etc using the same process for visualisation as was previously described in the section on Visualisation. The emphasis will be on the beautiful and on the umlaut on the 'o' – 'ö'. The word 'schon' can be dealt with separately with the student visualising an empty plate where the food (cake) has already been eaten. There is nothing left but the crumbs. Visualise the empty plate with the empty round 'o' with nothing on top!

schön   **schon**

ein schöner Kuchen   **schon gegessen**

"In the middle of the plate is the letter 'o'. What has happened to the food (cake) that was on the plate? – It has **already** been eaten. What is the letter you see on the plate? – That's right, it's a plain 'o' with nothing on top". Ensure the student looks at the picture till they have a clear picture before looking up to a blank bit of wall to the left. You can then ascertain if they have a clear picture in their mind.

Visualisation is useful too for spelling of any words that are tricky. Once students learn to visualise for themselves they can start to do the whole technique themselves. It is also important to get the learners to make up their own visual image which they try to remember. They will need help at the start to understand the process and to think of the type of thing that will promote visualisation and learning but once the technique is mastered it can be extremely helpful to the memory process and learning.

Colour may help many students to remember gender, so they may colour the definite and indefinite articles for feminine nouns in red, masculine in blue and neuter in brown. It doesn't matter which colour they choose, but it must be consistent or the technique won't work.

An example of a starter for some feminine Spanish words for clothing might be:

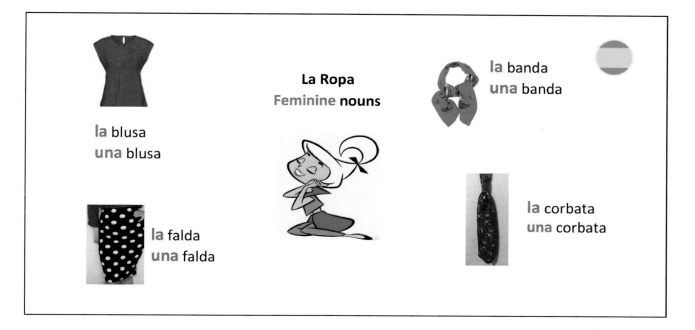

Students can make up their own examples once they have a starter and should draw their own pictures for given themes. They don't have to be artistic, just draw their own picture, cartoon or choose a computer image, but once they have been shown they should do this for themselves.

Similarly for masculine definite and indefinite articles for Spanish clothing terms.

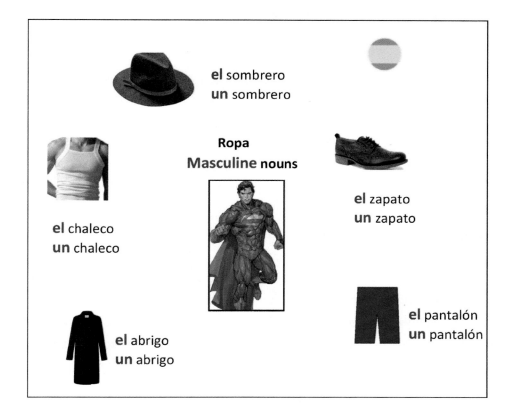

German neuter gender:

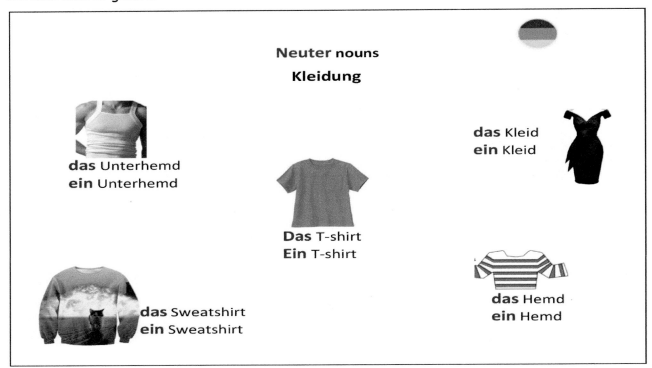

Neuter nouns
Kleidung

das Unterhemd
ein Unterhemd

Das T-shirt
Ein T-shirt

das Kleid
ein Kleid

das Sweatshirt
ein Sweatshirt

das Hemd
ein Hemd

The addition of colour and highlighting provide a visual stimulus that combined with other sensory experiences provided by the teacher or through the innovation of the pupil, promote learning.

Large print can help too, as can photocopying onto coloured paper. Those with dyslexia can have difficulties that are exacerbated by visual stress. This may mean that print is distorted when they see black print against a white background. The strong contrast is unhelpful and decoding becomes much easier when a coloured background is provided. Even if there has been no official diagnosis, the use of coloured paper for photocopying can make reading much more comfortable for many different learners. A neutral beige colour is usually best if you are unsure. Do confirm however that a referral is made for specialist help if visual problems are indicated and no assessment has been conducted. (See separate section – **Visual Stress** on page 148).

> Explanations need to be given concisely and will probably require to be repeated. If the student doesn't understand in the language they are learning, even when given very simply, then home language should be used for explanations, and repeated as often as is required.

Explanations need to be oral though giving a written backup is helpful. Learners with dyslexia are often very disheartened by seeing written comments on their work and they don't take time to read them, especially when reading is a chore. Encouragement and empathy can be conveyed in a simple explanation giving much needed support to the learners. Support needs to be given as unobtrusively as possible so that the learner feels comfortable to ask questions. Those with dyslexia often require more time due to their speed of processing. Speech does require to be slowed down to an unnatural speed to begin with, but once the learner 'catches on' it can be speeded up to a more natural speed.

For topics, giving a key wordlist – perhaps in the format above – or on cards with the word on one side and a picture on the other, can be very helpful and encourage the student to practise on their own till they reach automaticity. It is helpful if a podcast or recording of some kind can be made in advance so the student has a good model for pronunciation.

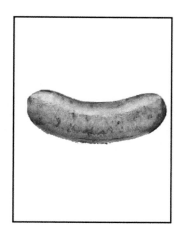

| **Front of Card** | **Back of Card** |

une saucisse

la saucisse

Buddying with another learner who is empathic towards the learner with dyslexia is helpful. The student can then practise speaking and listening in a safe environment. It is important not to put a learner with dyslexia 'on the spot'. They need the reassurance of knowing they won't be judged by other learners and won't be asked to read or speak out in a large group. Working in pairs or trios can work well but sensitive organisation is required to ensure all learners are benefiting.

The importance of technology should not be underestimated. Though language is of course a communicative subject, the repeated presentations of vocabulary and phrases that the learner needs, can be tedious to the person listening. A computer can provide a patient helper which never tires of listening. Though not a substitute for a real living companion, it can provide the much needed practice without tedium to a human listener. Close supervision is needed to ensure that the learner is responding appropriately. In a classroom situation a computer or listening bank cannot replace the teacher. It can however be an excellent helper. Video, MP3s, downloads, computer, tablet, phone and appropriate software can back up the teaching in a potentially welcome way giving the overlearning needed. However even the technology can be made more multisensory by the introduction of novel ways of bringing in sensory stimuli.

Modelling is necessary for all learners and the wider the variety of techniques used to provide a good model the better. The Language Master ® System can provide a useful model that learners can use to practise phrases and words. The machine is a card reader which provides multi-sensory experiences for learners as they can see, hear, speak and then listen to the teacher and get instant feedback through hearing their own voice played back. Teachers can design their own cards to match the level and vocabulary to the learner's needs.

Mnemonic strategies should be encouraged and be designed to suit the learners' circumstances. Labelling furniture with sticky notes, colour-coding gender words, placing picture cards with vocabulary where learners can readily see them will help. Similarly mini white boards can be used to draw, label and make sentences that can easily be erased and changed if there are errors. Along with the use of technology these are all ways of giving overlearning and reinforcement.

When speaking, provide students with 'wait time' to allow for their slower speed of processing information. This is exacerbated by having to translate before replying. Support learners as unobtrusively as possible to give them confidence to speak out. Instead of penfriends, a Skype pal or e-friend can encourage like-minded individuals to find a purpose and reason to use and improve their language. Such approaches are likely to help all young people, but for those with dyslexia, they are really necessary to promote learning. Likewise multi-sensory learning helps all but not everyone will really need it. Those with dyslexia will.

Benefits of Multisensory teaching

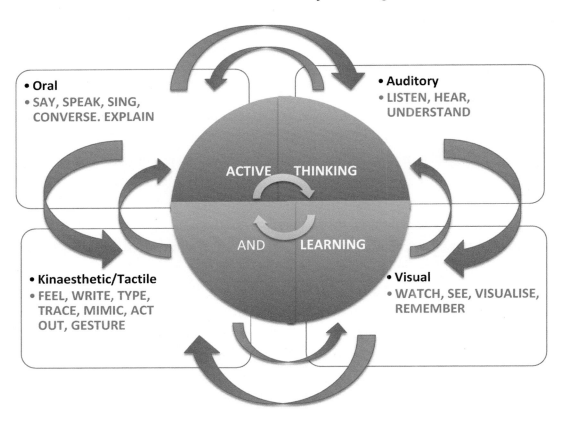

Diagrams, mind mapping, and concept mapping are all useful strategies that are illustrated in this section and described in more detail at various points in the book. The following summarises concisely what we can do in relation to language learning.

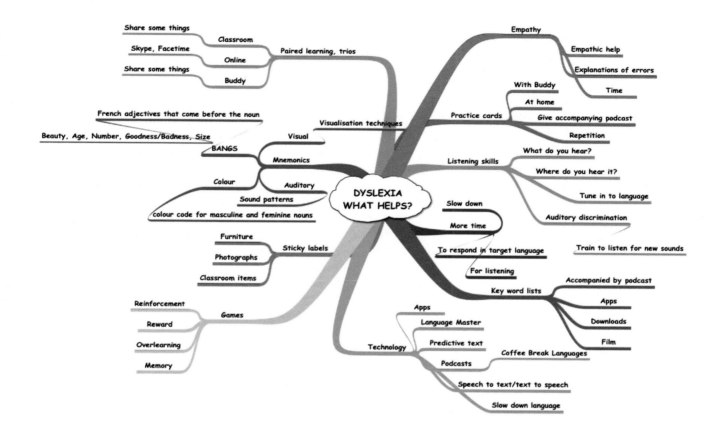

In language learning, as in other areas, the use of technology can have great benefits. While all students are likely to benefit from technology, for those with dyslexia technology can prove a patient teacher giving opportunities for overlearning, self-correction and multisensory learning. Further suggestions for the use of technology are given in the appendices along with useful websites.

Chapter 11

Support in other Curriculum Areas

The Expressive Arts

There is absolutely no reason to believe that children and young people with dyslexia are in any way different from other children in respect of artistic talent and design skills. On the contrary, there is some evidence to suggest that those with dyslexia are superior on skills such as artistic design, modelling and architecture. The elements that those with dyslexia are likely to find difficult will be in reading and writing about their subject, and approaches to these skills should be multisensory and use strategies previously discussed. Where appropriate, reasonable adjustments may require to be made to ensure arrangements are in place in class and for examinations. Technology can be used to circumvent the need for a human reader and writer.

As one might expect, those with specific learning difficulties may have more trouble in learning musical notation and in reading a score, but eventually, as with reading a book, the skills can be mastered and the child can become extremely successful in this field. Strategies of colour coding notes can be tried out but may not work for everyone. Those with visual perceptual difficulties might find that colouring the middle line of a stave will improve visual processing. Break down the learning of pieces of music into short sections to give immediate positive feedback and allow lots of time for practice. Most of all, ensure learning is multisensory and encourage the student to sing along to help reinforce the pattern and rhythm of the music.

Planning may be a problem in such activities, but if learners are encouraged to draw up their own timetable and stick to deadlines, they should be able to cope well. There is further information on this in the Chapter 12 - **Improving Support across the Curriculum**.

The Sciences

No special programmes are necessary in this area. Students with dyslexia are generally as capable as others, with the main difficulties lying when there are considerable amounts of written work involved. It is sufficient to say that the same principles apply to this as to other areas. Accommodations are often required to circumvent the difficulties of writing and reading as described previously. Help for skills of organisation and planning along with curriculum-supportive approaches are given in Chapter 12.

If there are memory or attention difficulties as might be encountered when there is an executive functioning difficulty, then automaticity may be facilitated by the use of probe sheets which set out vocabulary to be mastered. This could also be used for the spelling of tricky words. This could be used in almost any subject though this one relates to science vocabulary. It is useful if a game approach is used to help establish the meaning of the words before testing. For example, once the words have been taught in school, then using a Pairs card game or Pelmanism with the meaning on one piece of card and the word on another can be helpful. With the blank side up, the cards are turned over two at a time till a match is gained. You would require a set of around ten words for this. Below is a probe sheet relating to physics, a blank master suitable for any subject is on the CD.

Name: _____		Subject: **Science**			
Keywords for **Energy and Electricity** Date:					
dynamo	*Meaning*: a machine for converting mechanical energy into electrical energy, typically by means of rotating coils of copper wire in a magnetic field.				
	Mon	Tues	Wed	Thurs	Fri
electromagnet	*Meaning*: a soft metal core made into a magnet by the passage of electric current through a coil surrounding it.				
	Mon	Tues	Wed	Thurs	Fri
voltage	*Meaning*: an electromotive force or potential difference expressed in volts				
	Mon	Tues	Wed	Thurs	Fri
voltmeter	*Meaning*: an instrument for measuring electric potential in volts.				
	Mon	Tues	Wed	Thurs	Fri
etc. etc.					

A further plan could revisit the words after a week, a month, etc. This is very useful also for establishing foreign language vocabulary to the point of automaticity. Games which involve matching pictures and words can be used for reinforcement of vocabulary for a whole range of subjects.

Credit should be given for oral responses and the opportunity taken to encourage as much participation as possible. If it is intended to include a significant amount of reading and the child is still having problems with this, then pair the child with a good reader of similar academic ability and allow them to work together, or make use of reading (text to speech) technology to ensure the learner is not disadvantaged. It will help also if a range of books is available to suit all ability levels, so some easy-read books should be available to cover topic areas.

Social Studies

Children and young people with dyslexia should be no different to other young people in regard to their understanding of the subjects involved in Social Studies. However it is likely they will require support for their reading and writing to enable them to fully participate. Providing information through digitally downloaded material such as podcasts that can be listened to, and the provision of teachers' notes as well as the other strategies previously described are likely to be helpful and enable full participation. It is essential however that these accommodations are put in place in the classroom and that when appropriate examination arrangements are applied for in good time so that students can show their abilities and understanding.

Religious and moral education

Access to written texts may prove problematic for young people with dyslexia if accommodations, are not put in place early. However with these accommodations that are likely to include downloaded versions of texts and books, and a willingness in classroom situations to accept oral rather than written answers, students should be able to participate and enjoy the subject matter.

Technologies

Technologies are likely to prove stimulating for young people with dyslexia and should be no different to other young people in regard to their understanding. Planning and organisation of course may require support. The practical aspects of the subject matter however should be areas in which young people with dyslexia can thrive and excel if they are motivated. There is no evidence from the research to suggest that dyslexia negatively affects the three-dimensional aspects of design, graphics, craft, etc. and many young people with dyslexia do excel in these areas.

Chapter 12

Improving Support
Across the Curriculum

Memory

In studying profiles of children with dyslexia, one aspect stands out as being particularly relevant. While all children are different and have varying patterns of strengths and difficulties, one reasonably constant factor is the very restricted ability that children with dyslexia have to use short-term and working memory. Presenting the child with a string of letters or digits at a speed of one per second, and asking the child to recall these can gain an easy assessment of the child's short-term and working memory span. Similarly presenting a string of letters or digits and getting the child to reverse the sequence can estimate working memory. While short-term memory only requires recall, working memory requires the learner to actively remember and reverse the sequence. Start with two items and increase these one at a time. If a child has a working memory span of only three items, it can be clearly seen why they have difficulty in remembering sequences of letters for spelling and sequences of instructions. The concept of working memory should not be confused with long term or event memory, as those are not generally affected. In practice this means that while the individual with dyslexia can remember every detail of a 'day-out' she had last year, she may not be able to remember three digits in sequence only a few seconds after she has been presented with them. When given sequential instructions, she may only be able to carry out two or three at a time. Working memory however can be improved with training. As for other areas, it is a matter of increasing the challenge in small increments and emphasising the progress gained.

Increasing the number of items that are to be remembered can be encouraged by getting the child to lay out plastic or wooden letters of the alphabet in an arc in front of him as previously described on page 72.

abcdefghijklmnopqrstuvwxyz

The activity of laying out the alphabet in order may in itself take some time to master, but will prove a worthwhile memory and sequencing exercise. Initially, if two or three children are having difficulty they can be grouped with a child who is able to help. Each child should however be given a chance to practise on her own and prove that she can manage it.

To improve auditory skills a sequence of letters is given, starting with around three and aiming to build up to around seven. The pupil listens, repeats the sequence, and then pulls out the letters from the arc. The child must learn to use strategies as an aid to memory, e.g. she may group the items in twos or threes. A more difficult task is to present the sequence in jumbled order but ask the child to display it in alphabetical order. The length of time between presenting the sequence and asking for recall can gradually be increased by about five second intervals. As memory span increases, an intervening task can be given between presentation and recall. With older children who have mastered alphabet sequencing, the plastic or wooden letters can be dispensed with and the letters written out.

Mnemonic strategies should be encouraged as an aid to remembering sequences of letters. For example, when given the sequence of random letters FMPTW, the child may think up a mnemonic such as "**F**unny **M**innie **P**uts **T**oys in **W**ellies". Visualisation in this case would be encouraged.

This technique can be used for remembering sequences for facts that should be remembered. A classic for this is the "Richard Of York gained battles in vain" mnemonic for remembering the colours of the rainbow - Red, Orange, Yellow, Green, Blue, Indigo, Violet. Instead of a list of letters, the children can be asked to remember a list of facts or items related to other work in the curriculum. Similar strategies are encouraged.

For visual memory, training can be given as before, but this time the items to be remembered should be presented visually. The important principle is to ensure that the tasks are presented so that success is achieved most, but not all, of the time. If the child constantly experiences failure, he will quickly cease to enjoy or benefit from such activities.

With younger children games will help. Games such as, 'I went to the shop (market) and bought ....' will help auditory sequential memory. Kim's Game in various forms and Pelmanism will help visual memory. The use of gesture as an aid to auditory sequential memory should be encouraged so that each part of the sequence has a specific movement that acts as a memory aid. This is particularly useful for learning poetry or other material that lends itself to forms of dramatisation. The teacher demonstrates the actions and the children copy while saying the poem or narrative.

For children having difficulty in learning sequences, such as the months of the year, it may help if they make a set of cards with a visual clue of their own choosing to associate with the month: For example:

Birthday month – April
with a picture of a birthday cake

Christmas – December
with a picture of a Christmas tree

Sequential memory skills can also be improved by adopting a games approach; e.g. the teacher holds up the name of a month and the children respond with the one after – or before. Children can sequence jumbled cartoon pictures into their right order and then tell the story as it should be.

Using mnemonic strategies as a memory aid, children should be encouraged to think up their own. These can be used to help in all areas of the curriculum. Visualisation techniques will probably help most children. They can be encouraged to imagine whatever they are aiming to remember in larger than life situations. Memory research has shown that the more unusual we imagine an item to be, the more likely we are to remember it. For example, if we wish the child to remember how to spell a word such as **BEAUTIFUL**, allow him to devise a mnemonic such as '**B**ig **E**lephants **A**re **U**nusually **T**imid **I**n **F**ollowing **U**seless **L**ions'. The more ridiculous the mnemonic, the more likely it is to be retained. Encourage the use of both mnemonic and visualisation techniques – if possible both together.

Big Elephants Are Unusually Timid In Following Useless Lions

The main point here is that memory can be improved for all children, not just those with dyslexia. Teaching strategies for memorisation need not be confined to one or two children. Starting points will vary as will increments, but the principles for improving memory can be applied to all. Visualisation is a useful approach for children to master as early as possible, for more details see **Visualisation** on page 94.

There are lots of other ways you can work on memory. Tony Buzan, for example, has written prolifically on the subject and suggests different strategies and approaches to memory training. Each strategy can be taught in around ten minutes, and your students can then practise and tell you how they find the strategy.

Memory of course does not always have to rely on mastering strategies. Mobile phones can act as reminders by remembering diary dates and times with audible alarms when something is due, or when the reminder is set to jog the memory. Similarly intelligent personal assistants for a reasonable cost (certainly considerably more economical than a human personal assistant) can set reminders, and provided there is a Wi-Fi signal, will operate with considerable patience and understanding! Also the camera of a Smartphone can be used to create a lasting image of something that has to be remembered. While there is a cost and technical devices cannot completely substitute for human memory they can act as huge support to it. Technology has of course to be used responsibly and thus needs some training to ensure this is the case.

Making Texts Accessible

For young people with dyslexia, handwritten notes are probably not to be recommended unless they are for a 'one-off' and are clear and legible. Notes, summaries and worksheets are best to be word-processed and must be to a high standard. They should not be photocopied to the point where they have faded and become difficult to read. Once a resource is made, it can be saved and kept for other situations. In this way the text can be adapted – font and size changed, colour added or taken away. Graphics can be inserted and dates or times can be changed to whatever is appropriate. In addition they can be printed on whatever colour of paper is considered most appropriate, particularly if a young person has visual stress.

Once a file has been created digitally that file can then be converted, using text-to-speech software to an audio file that the student can listen to if reading is a problem. They can then listen at a time and place that suits and if using earphones, no one need ever know what it is they are listening to.

If students are to be expected to read the text, then check it is at a suitable level. A learner with dyslexia may well be reading two years or more behind their chronological age so it is important to ensure the text is at the right level so it can be read.

If using Word, the readability level can easily be checked. Some other points to consider are:

- Would the use of a bulleted or numbered list make things simpler and easier to follow?
- Would the addition of a graphic or illustration help?
- Are there technical words that might need to be explained?
- Would a flow chart or diagram help to illustrate how something works?
- Use Bold print to emphasise key words.
- Ensure print is not too dense. If it seems it might be, then split up text by inserting more paragraph breaks and the inclusion of lists if appropriate.
- Would a summary at the beginning or end help?

Establish which fonts are preferred if the child is old enough to know. Otherwise test out different fonts and sizes and measure the amount of time it takes the child to read and consider the effect on comprehension.

> There are however a few fonts which are claimed to be more dyslexia-friendly than others - *Comic Sans*, Dyslexie, **Lexie Readable**, Century Gothic and Arial are all fonts which do not have a serif and which many people with dyslexia prefer. However, it is probably best to ask the learners if in doubt.

In a word-processed document the Format/Paragraph command can be used to add space (from 1 point upwards) before or after a single paragraph, a group of paragraphs or all in the document. It can also be used to set line spacing so the text is not too dense.

Text should not be justified and should be aligned to the left of the page. Many people with dyslexia (and some without) report that the spaces between words in justified text makes it seem that the white spaces are like rivers of white flowing down the page. The contrast between the font colour and the background should not be of too high a contrast. Black print on a beige background is generally found to be more readable than black on white. This can be the preferred option for the whole class and whole school.

For computer use, consider background colour and text colour and ensure that the student is aware of how to change the colour to suit his needs. As well as adjusting text and background colour, it is possible to adjust the colour temperature or tint of a screen to make the overall colour cast warmer or, more usually, colder and bluer. If using shared computers then again, the student will need to be aware of how to do (and undo) this. Consider also line spacing. It is quite likely that students prefer 1.5 line spacing.

Accessibility to books can often be gained by having a PDF file of the book and PDF reader. WordTalk is a free text reader for Microsoft Word. Project Gutenberg and Google Books have PDFs of many out of copyright English Literature canon that are free to download.

More modern books are available from Amazon as Kindle Whispersync which synchronises text on a computer (or tablet) screen with recorded audio if available and computerised Text to Speech otherwise.

Apple VoiceOver will read anything on a screen (computer, iPad or iPhone) and works well with PDFs and material published on Apple iBooks which includes many books in the English Literature syllabus.

Visual Stress

Visual stress should not be confused with dyslexia but it does need to be considered if there is a possibility a learner is unable to read at the speed and fluency they should. Visual stress refers to the symptoms of discomfort that distort visual perception when attempting to read. Visual stress can occur for a variety of reasons, but as a result, reading is often slowed down and can result in headaches and apparently distorted print that may appear to move around on the page.

Visual stress can result in a lowering of self-esteem and motivation to keep on with the reading process. The problems require a practising optometrist to diagnose them. However teachers and others should be aware of the signs of visual stress and refer on if in doubt. Problems can often be addressed through the use of tinted spectacles and/or overlays. A specialist however is necessary to ensure correct diagnosis and rule out any more serious problems.

Some young people with dyslexia require to have text printed on coloured paper if they have visual stress. Spectacles with a specific tint are the most effective solution as then students do not need to carry an overlay with them and can read from any book or worksheet.

Learning Styles

All individuals have learning needs and it is important to consider these. While it is not always possible in a classroom situation to teach according to individual needs we should be aware of those and individualise our teaching if and when necessary. The need to look at metacognitive approaches and teaching students to take control of their own learning quite naturally leads to investigating learning styles and consideration of each learner as an individual with their own needs. With good planning, even in a classroom situation, knowledge of how students learn best will help us plan to meet the needs of all students.

> Often a student with dyslexia will have a holistic, global style of learning which does not always respond well to the sequential, analytic way of teaching which many teachers adopt.

This may mean the individual with dyslexia will see things from a central focus and then work out to the seemingly less important factors, or they may see the separate parts of a topic before being able to see how they fit into a logical sequence.

When applied to planning a piece of writing, it may be more logical to start planning with a central idea and then build other ideas around that central point. Encouraging mind mapping can be helpful for any pupils who prefer to start with the main idea. The addition of colour to a mind map will give an added dimension that may act as an aide memoire. The following is an example of a student's mind map on computers.

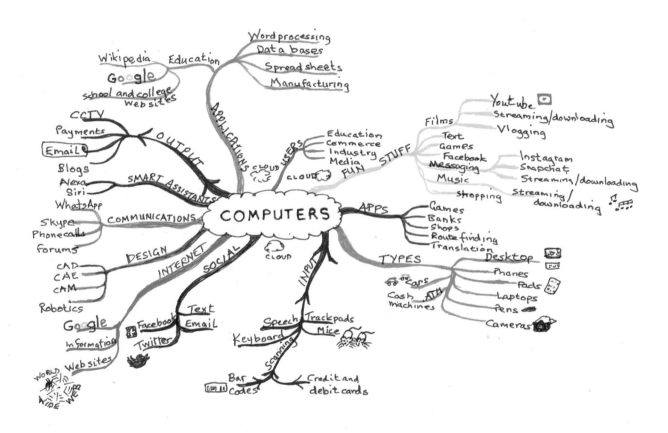

Over recent years, questions have been raised about the efficacy of teaching according to learning styles theory, and much of this theory has been seen as questionable. This apart, there are undoubtedly benefits to be gained from considering for example, seating arrangements of children and young people who find sitting still problematic and need to move around a lot. It is best to seat children who are restless and need to move around constantly on the periphery of the classroom where they can move without disrupting the other students in the classroom. They can unobtrusively be given tasks to do throughout the day without disturbing other children and they can come to see the teacher with minimal disruption. The responsibility of carrying out duties for the teacher may also act as an incentive to learning. Children who have attention difficulties and hyperactivity will benefit from having their needs viewed sympathetically and taken into account when planning strategies that will affect the whole class.

We must take care however that responding to individual learning needs does not take control of the classroom. We may end up pandering to individual children's whims rather than truly teaching to individual needs. We can go a long way towards teaching children in the way they learn best, but teachers must always keep control of the situation.

Thinking skills

Thinking skills refer to the mental processing that helps us make sense of our experiences. Thinking skills help us to integrate new information into our existing schema as we build and deepen our understanding in a way that helps us to apply new ideas, consider possibilities and evaluate our choices before making decisions. As such, thinking skills are important. They can be encouraged and developed in all children and are best promoted in a group situation. Most of our children do not understand how they learn best and encouraging them to think about what works for them in learning can promote the development of more effective metacognitive strategies. Thinking skills and metacognition are areas where much further research is needed. Though there is agreement on the need to promote better thinking and learning, there is currently very little consensus on how best to promote such approaches in schools.

A number of specific courses are available designed to promote thinking skills. With young people in the school situation it is important that they learn to relate skills to the curriculum and are encouraged to think 'out of the box' while ensuring learning. Techniques and consideration of various perspectives on thinking can be discussed in the classroom but should not be limited to any single approach. Creativity and inventiveness should be encouraged in all learners so that young people learn to understand that different ways of thinking are desirable. Thinking must be at the heart of the curriculum and though young people with dyslexia will have areas of weakness, thinking should not be one. Often young people with dyslexia will find innovative ways of doing things, analysing, synthesising and evaluating for themselves. Learning how to transfer learning from one area to others and to adapt as various external factors change is vital for future learning. The skills that today's young people will require will be considerably different in many ways from those which their teachers felt to be important when they were at school.

For young people with dyslexia, thinking skills and metacognitive approaches are particularly important as reading and comprehension may have been delayed by early difficulties. Approaches such as those described previously for reciprocal teaching should be promoted within a group context with a view to increasing competence and confidence and encouraging all young people to take more control over their own learning. The process of asking questions, clarifying information, summarising and then predicting what will happen from consideration of the circumstances, can guide and deepen the thinking of the young people and give them the confidence to make an effort when learning is a struggle for them.

Questioning using the word, 'how' can be very helpful. "How could I do this, how could I do it differently, how would it work if.........?" etc. These skills are important for all, but it is particularly important that those with dyslexia see themselves as every bit as good as those without dyslexia when it comes to thinking and solving problems.

Digital Assistive Technology

Along with carefully focused teaching, the use of digital assistive technology can have a major impact on the ability of young people to thrive in the classroom and study situation – something that without the appropriate technological support they would be unable to do. Assistive technology, when it is used as a reasonable adjustment as the learner's normal way of working in the classroom, can also support examination arrangements.

Computer software and apps provide patient, non-judgemental means of reinforcing almost any task where overlearning and repetition are going to be important. The facility to set work at students' levels and then to obtain a printout of results means that tasks can be completed, then revised with minimum of teaching and supervision. A vast array of material is available to suit a range of needs. Where possible it is best to try out software before purchase and many companies with expensive programs can arrange trial versions of software for prospective purchasers. Young people generally enjoy the games element of technology and it is worth evaluating material for them from a pedagogic perspective as well as evaluating the material with them to ensure it is fun to play before buying.

The use of word processors has been mentioned previously and the benefits to students with dyslexia and literacy difficulties are very obvious to anyone comparing handwritten and word-processed work. A number of predictive word processors are available which will 'learn' words that the young person uses and store them in a dictionary, building up the vocabulary of words which the student uses most often. As the student types, the program predicts what the word is likely to be, thus reducing the amount of typing necessary. Programs such as *Lightkey* can be downloaded at no cost and these not only cut the number of key strokes necessary to produce the work, they also amend spelling if it is comprehensible, resulting in an overall improved presentation.

Some students like predictive software; others find the programs themselves to be a distraction from the flow of words. For some they are a great asset while for others they are a hindrance. It may be worth persisting but it does have to be established if the student is sufficiently able to identify the words being presented. If not, then it may be best to leave for a while before re-trying. If it is likely that predictive text will be useful for the student then it will be best to arrange a trial so the student can evaluate for herself how best to use the software.

Spoken output from programs such as *Write:Outloud* enables students to gain auditory feedback on what they have typed into the computer and lets them know when an inappropriate or misspelled word has been used. The spelling checker will speak out mis-spellings and the student will then recognise when a wrong word has been used and can amend. This immediate feedback helps develop the relationship between the written word and the correct spelling. The program can also import other files so they can be read back. It is worth considering font size, colour and speech options so the student gains maximum benefit.

Scanning pens, such as the *C-Pen*, offer a reading tool that students can use to read words aloud. They give increased independence to learners with dyslexia and there is a version that can be used in the classroom and examination situation. The pen uses optical character recognition (OCR). When scanned across text it will read back what is written. It can speak slowly and also offers a dictionary function that will define words a student is unclear about. It will file data and the data can be transferred to a computer or tablet. The facility to read words back on demand has been found to be a great asset to those with dyslexia. The device can be customised to the individual student and leads to greater independence. It is not however suitable for everyone so it is again worth trialling this with the student before buying. Devices can be very useful for students who are learning English as an additional language as they let them know how the word is pronounced. Used with headphones, it is possible for a candidate to take the Exam Reader pen into the examination situation feeling confident that any words they are unsure of can be read out to them without the need for human intervention.

Programs such as *Clicker* provide writing support for pupils and can give literacy support across the curriculum. The program can be customised for individual children so they gain greater accessibility. The program will speak back what the children have written so if there are misspellings, these are likely to be recognised when the computer reads back the material. It contains a library of pictures to enhance the students' writing and will also predict what students wish to say.

Voice or speech recognition systems such as *Voice Type* and *Dragon* enable students to speak and have their speech appear on the computer screen. They avoid the need for typing and writing and can be used in the classroom as well as in examinations. Typing skills aren't relevant and this means the student is freed from worrying about spelling and typing. The student can therefore concentrate on the matters in hand. The software quickly learns to recognise the learner's voice and very little training is needed to produce the desired text. It is however not suitable for use in a very noisy environment. For examinations a separate room is generally needed to ensure noise is kept down and that the computer is able to reproduce the text the learner wishes with the minimum of corrections.

Electronic communications such as web browsers, email and texting are all methods of communicating information. There are different expectations and standards of presentation in all the various forms of digital communications.

Predictive text can help those with dyslexia if they are able to identify the right word and will often be the preferred option when sending a message by text. Social media with its acceptance of film, use of emoticons and photo too can be a good option and empower the youngster with dyslexia. Communication in the digital age should not be allowed to set young people with dyslexia apart from others. Success is about finding the right means of communicating and using it to everyone's advantage.

For finding information from websites there is speech output available. For those computers that don't have speech built in, it can be accessed without much additional work. However personal assistants such as *Siri* and *Alexa* can be the answer for anyone with severe dyslexia and difficulty in accessing written information. Even for those with no difficulties, the technology is such that it is fast becoming the easiest way of accessing information – from train timetables to the meaning of life! What is clear is that technology is not standing still and is becoming increasingly available and accessible in hand-held devices. With developments progressing at the current rate there should be no reason for young people being unable to access information on whatever subject and in whichever format they wish.

Many local authorities have their own services to advise on assistive technology. *AbilityNet* is a charity that advises on technology and how it can best be used to help those with disabilities to overcome these disabilities and achieve their goals. In Scotland, *CALL Scotland* provides information and advice on technological aids for communication and learning to professionals, carers and disabled people themselves. There is no 'one size fits all', but both websites have a wealth of information in an accessible format that can be accessed from anywhere.

Motivation

Motivation has been mentioned at various points previously. It does however warrant a separate paragraph due to its importance to the learning situation. An individual who lacks motivation, dyslexic or not, is unlikely to learn much. While this book promotes early intervention as the best method of preventing demotivation, there are unfortunately cases where dyslexia goes unrecognised in the early years. It is therefore critical that the young person with dyslexia who has previously met failure in much of what he has attempted, be presented with material in such a way that errors and failures are minimised and priority given to maximising his success rate. This will build confidence and encourage the child to persist in tasks that have proved easy for other children of similar ability level. Make use of the child's strengths in order to encourage and exercise the areas of weakness.

Praise should be used frequently and opportunities taken to improve the child's self-image and esteem. Praise however does require to be genuine so tasks must be geared to the right level so children do achieve success and praise can genuinely be given.

On occasion, the child's lack of understanding of his own difficulties will exacerbate the low self-esteem and lack of motivation he seems to display and lead to anxiety. The child or young person may not want to go to school or may have tummy aches on days when there is a test. This can lead to the child saying, "I can't do it" without considering the reason and using dyslexia as an excuse when this may not be the case. If this is not tackled at an early stage it can lead to later problems of negative stress with possible effects on mental health and lack of motivation generally for any work tasks.

To bring about the desired change in attitude, it is best that someone who understands the child's difficulties fully explains to him the nature of his learning challenges, and so decreases the fear of failure. Differing abilities, learning styles and interests should be set in a personalised context and positive role models discussed. We also need to ensure that this is a consistent message and that negative images are not being portrayed elsewhere in the child's environment – in other classrooms, the playground or home. Giving the child more of something they have previously failed in will not help. We must avoid the defensive strategy of 'not trying' for fear of failure. Through the promotion of positive imagery, we strive to ensure growth mindset.

Ensuring a growth mindset

Encouraging a growth mindset, is about fostering the belief that we can all learn and get better, no matter what our difficulties and strengths. Praising young people for the effort they make is more likely to produce successful learners and effective contributors than leading youngsters to believe that they have, or don't have, a disability and a lack of capacity to learn. The reality that those with dyslexia do have difficulties in some areas is acknowledged.

> We must however encourage children to find and then develop their best ways of learning, building new beliefs through a metacognitive approach. We must encourage experimenting with the different strategies and approaches we offer so that the learner understands that if one method doesn't work, it isn't the final word on the matter. There are always ways round or through a problem that are different. We just need to find these ways.

The old adage that if young people can't learn the way we teach, then we must teach the way they learn suggests that if we are prepared to value different ways of thinking about problems, we and the learners will gain a positive experience from which all will benefit. By praising effort and considering the methods learners choose to use in tackling problems (whether we consider them to be good or not) lets youngsters know that there is more than one way of getting a right answer and though their answers may not always be right, their innovation of methodology is appreciated. This means the child is more willing to put in an effort the next time a problem arises. When children are put down for getting wrong answers they soon lose the willingness to make an effort, and then a label of dyslexia can indeed become a self-fulfilling prophesy of failure. Getting a wrong answer is about gaining a learning opportunity rather than failing.

A consistent culture of high expectation and quality feedback is more likely to give all learners the motivation for successful learning in spite of their difficulties. Feedback should entail asking, "What are you aiming to achieve (What's your target?)", "How are you getting on (What progress are you making towards your target?)", and "What do you plan to do next to take you closer to your target or to reach your target?" This questioning should of course be made specific to the tasks in hand. In time it should be done by the young person himself who will learn to plan and evaluate his own learning. It must be encouraged however in a positive framework considering carefully the challenges and how these can be overcome, and the young person's answers must be positively framed by the person asking the questions.

Showing learners pictures of famous dyslexics is one suggestion for ensuring a growth mindset, but learners must understand that Richard Branson, Jamie Oliver, Whoopie Goldberg or whichever individual we highlight were not born successful. They had to take responsibility for their own development and achievement at some point. Though there were people who helped them along the way, they were still responsible for fulfilling the innate potential that they had. They had a growth mindset.

Prior to assessment and immediately after first realising they are dyslexic many young people view dyslexia as something negative that will preordain a future of failure. Explaining to children how their brains work and that new connections can be made in the brain through appropriate learning and practice encourages young people to grow their talents. Having a growth mindset leads to the view that over time young people can learn to believe in themselves in a way that helps them cope with the inevitable setbacks. In this way youngsters begin to understand that they do have control over their own destiny and that dyslexia does not preordain a future of failure as they has assumed. With effort and support, young people can develop and train their brains.

Learners with dyslexia often fear learning new things, believing they won't be able to do them before they even start. This fear is very real and built on past experience. However it is very negative and it may take time to build that student's self-belief.

> If all students stop themselves from saying, "I can't do it", and only allow themselves to say, "I can't manage this **yet**", they learn to think more positively and ask, "What can I do?" and give themselves permisison to ask questions and tell the teacher that there are bits they don't understand.

They need to be able to trust in getting an empathic response. Fear of ridicule and failure in children must be overcome, and with the right approach from teachers, students can gain a positive growth mindset. Learners must come to recognise when they are viewing their own development from a fixed viewpoint and change that to a growth mindset. Seeing intelligence (whatever that might be) as fixed is entirely wrong, though indeed that is often what our students with dyslexia do believe. They see others as having an innate ability to read, write and spell which they don't have. So feedback to all children is vital in encouraging the growth mindset we want to achieve.

It is more helpful to say:

> "I see how you've done that."
>
> "You remembered to use ……. to help. That was a good strategy."
>
> "You've made a really good effort to work this out, and you've managed to ……….
>
> Now here's what you can do to finish off (or whatever),"

showing that you really appreciate the effort the children have made and leading them to a belief in their own abilities to get the job done. Instead of thinking, "I can't do this," we can change their view to, "I just need to learn how to do this" or "I haven't managed this – YET!"

Encouraging a growth mindset is something that should not be limited to those with additional needs. All young people can benefit from teachers who have high expectations and can give them feedback on new and realistic strategies that are likely to help. Having the belief that their learning can change through acting on feedback improves self-esteem and reduces feelings of helplessness. Many young people with dyslexia believe they are unintelligent. Teaching children to talk themselves through tasks in a positive way, asking, "What did I do well?", "How did I manage to get those all right?" and "I can do this" helps reduce stress and aggression and builds self-belief.

Almost all children can learn to read though it may take longer and be a much greater struggle for those with dyslexia than it is for others. It may not be easy but helping children and young people to develop a growth mindset and to believe in themselves is crucial in leading young people to change their outlook in the ways needed to pave the way to future success.   A growth mindset requires persistence, and refusing to dwell on failure, but focusing on how problems can be solved.

> The message to the young people must be, "Don't give up –
> find another way if the first doesn't work for you!"

The CD contains a list of 20 things to do to provide effective feedback and promote a growth mindset.

Working With Parents

Perhaps the most important resource in helping and supporting students with dyslexia is parental involvement. Parents/carers know their children. They are with them for much more time than they are at school. Parents want to be involved and want to know what school and teachers are doing. Intervention and support work best when teachers, parents and any other specialists work together. It is worth spending time with parents to ensure they are fully aware of what school is doing, and what they can do to support school, and their child at home. Often teachers are unaware of how long it takes the young person with dyslexia to do their homework in the evening.

When students are tired, what should take ten minutes can take an hour and a half. Parents can become very frustrated resulting in stress all round. Parents, particularly of primary school children should agree a reasonable time for children to spend on homework, and once that is exceeded, then a note in the child's jotter or an email to the teacher (if that is the preferred method of communicating) should be sufficient to explain why homework was not finished.

Sometimes it may be sufficient for parents to read books so the children grow up appreciating stories, but at other times more help is required. It is important for teachers to understand if parents do themselves have difficulties with reading and spelling, as often these difficulties are hereditary. It may be that teachers can recommend a good app or book that will help for parents to use with children at home. If the child is on a specialist teacher's programme (and even if not), then a short practice of word attack, phonics and reading following a specific structured programme each night may be very productive.

Parents may be able to help in ways that they had not previously considered. If a parent is dyslexic, they may have learned coping strategies or learning techniques that they can share with their child. Involving the parent in supporting their child may give that parent insight into the child's mind and increase their empathy and power to help. However this must be considered sensitively so the parent is not made to feel that they have a problem.

There are support organisations that can often help parental understanding of the difficulties and strengths of young people with dyslexia. Teachers can guide parents as to how to contact these organisations and where they meet. It is very easy when parents first realise their child is dyslexic to focus on the negative, but there is every reason to focus on the positives of dyslexia. It is helpful for young people to remember how many entrepreneurs, actors and actresses, millionaires, etc. are dyslexic, so dyslexia definitely does not mean that students are incapable of success. School may be hard for them, but when they find their niche in life, dyslexia can become a driving force for success. Help and support through the early and school years is vitally important in ensuring young people grow up with a 'can do' attitude rather than allowing dyslexia to predict failure.

Epilogue

The road to success for children and young people with dyslexia can be lengthy and sometimes tedious for all concerned. It cannot be travelled in haste or some will be lost by the wayside. For the teacher who has the patience to travel with the young person, adopt their pace, and accept the sometimes unconventional routes that accompany their learning, there are considerable rewards. To see the children reach their destination in spite of adversity and a difficult journey at times, is reward enough.

I hope this book has cast some light on the nature of difficulties encountered, and will act as a guide to class teachers on possible directions to follow. No one route is recommended for all as there are many profiles of dyslexia and many overlapping strengths and weaknesses which can co-exist. Just as every human being is different, every child and young person with dyslexia is different. It is important therefore that we do not look for one common pathway and direct our students down it, but that we hold a light to show a range of ways and multiple approaches that our students can evaluate and adopt as appropriate.

Those with dyslexia have many gifts to offer, as a glance at any gallery of famous dyslexics will attest. However many have smaller roles to play and they too need the focused teaching and support of teachers who can empathise and help them to reach their own destination. Their journey too is valuable. I hope the suggestions contained in this book will serve to highlight the possibilities and likely channels to allow those with dyslexia to reach their desired destination.

Bibliography

Alexander-Passe, N. (2015). **Dyslexia and Mental Health**. London: Jessica Kingsley Publishers.

Apel, K., Brimo, D., Diehm, E., & Apel, L. (2013). **Morphological awareness intervention with kindergartners and first- and second-grade students from low socioeconomic status homes: A feasibility study**. Language, Speech and Hearing Services in Schools, 44(2),161–173.

British Psychological Society. (1999). **Dyslexia, literacy and psychological assessment**. Report by Working Party of the Division of Educational and Child Psychology. Leicester: British Psychological Society.

Brooks, G. (2016). **What works for children and young people with literacy difficulties? The effectiveness of intervention schemes** (5th ed.). University of Sheffield: Dyslexia-SpLD Trust.

Buzan, T. (2002). **How to mind map**. London: Thorsons.

Cooper-Kahn, J. and Deitzel, L. (2008). **Late, lost and unprepared: A parents' guide to helping children with executive functioning**. Bethesda, MD: Woodbine House Inc.

Crombie, M. (1997). **Specific learning difficulties (dyslexia): A teachers' guide** (2nd ed.). Belford: Ann Arbor Publishers.

Crombie, M.A. (2002). D**yslexia – the new dawn: Policy, practice, provision and management of dyslexia from pre-five to primary**. Unpublished PhD thesis, Glasgow: University of Strathclyde.

Greenland, S.K. (2010). **The mindful child**. New York: Atria Books.

Harvard University Center on the Developing Child (2018). **Executive function and Self-regulation**. Available at http://developingchild.harvard.edu/science/key-concepts/executive-function/ , (accessed 2nd February 2018).

Jones, A. & Kindersley, K. (2013). **Dyslexia: Assessing and reporting: The Patoss Guide**. London: Hodder.

Johnson, B & Hagger-Johnson, G. (2013). **Psychometric assessment, statistics and report writing**. London: Pearson.

Kormos, J. & Smith, A.M. (2012). **Teaching languages to students with specific learning differences**. Bristol: Multilingual Matters.

Ozernov-Palchik, O., Norton, E.S., Sideridis, G., Beach, S.D., Wolf, M. Gabrieliand, J.D.E. & Gaab, N. (2017). **Longitudinal stability of pre-reading skill profiles of kindergarten children**. Developmental Science, 20(5), 1-18.

Palincsar, A.S. and Brown, A.L. (1984). **Reciprocal teaching of comprehension-fostering and comprehension-monitoring activities**. Cognition and Instruction, 1(2), 117 -175.

Rose, Sir J. (2009). **Identifying and teaching children and young people with dyslexia and literacy difficulties**: An independent report from Sir Jim Rose to the Secretary of State for children, schools and families. Nottingham: DCSF publications.

Schneider, E. & Crombie, M. (2003). **Dyslexia and foreign language learning**. London: David Fulton Publishers.

Scottish Government (2018). **Definition of dyslexia**. Available at http://www.addressingdyslexia.org/what-dyslexia (accessed 5th October 2018).

Snowling, M.J. & Hulme, C. (2011). **Evidence-based interventions for reading and language difficulites: Creating a virtuous circle**. British Journal of Educational Psychology, 81, 1-23.

Snowling, M.J. & Hulme, C. (2012). **Interventions for children's language and literacy difficulties**. International Journal of Language and Communication Disorders, 47(1), 27-34.

Topping, K. (1995). **Paired reading, spelling and writing: The handbook for teachers and parents**. London: Cassell.

Torgesen, J.K. (2002). **The prevention of reading difficulties**. Journal of School Psychology, 40(1), 7–26.

Watkins, G. & Hunter-Carsch, M. (1995). **Prompt spelling: A practical approach to paired spelling**. Support for Learning, 10(3), 133-138.

Wendon, T. (2018). **Letterland**. Available at https://www.letterland.com (accessed 5th October 2018).

Wolf, M. (2007). **Proust and the squid. The story of science and the reading brain**. New York, NY: HarperCollins Publishers.

Wolter, J.A., Wood, A. & D'zatko, K.W. (2009). **The influence of morphological awareness on the literacy development of first-grade children**. Language, Speech and Hearing Services in Schools. 40(3), 286-298.

APPENDIX 1

Assessment Material

This is a sample of what is available for the assessment of dyslexia. Many other tools could be used but along with a detailed analysis of free writing and the learner's literacy work in school, this would be more than adequate for establishing whether or not dyslexia is present. It is the responsibility of the assessor to ensure that the tools used are the most up-to-date available as the standardised scores lose their value as the materials go out of date. It is also wise to treat scores with caution if the standardisation was done in another country. There may be some cultural variation.

Barnett, A., Henderson, S.E., Scheib, B. & Schulz. J. (2007). **Detailed Assessment of Speed of Handwriting (DASH)**. London: Pearson Education.
Subtests examine fine motor and precision skills, the speed of producing well known written material, the ability to alter speed of performance on two tasks with identical content and free writing competency. For group or individual administration - suitable for ages 9 to 16:11.

Beery, K.E., Beery, N.A. & Buktenica, N.A. (2010). **Beery-Buktenica Developmental Test of Visual-Motor Integration** (6th ed.). London: Pearson Education.
Considers the extent to which individuals can integrate their visual and motor abilities.
For ages 2 to 100 years.

Caplan, M. Bark, C. & McLean, B. (2013) **Helen Arkell Spelling Test (HAST-2)** (2nd ed.). Surrey: Helen Arkell Dyslexia Centre.
Single word spelling for 5 years – Adult.

Dunn, L.M., Dunn, L.M. and Styles, B. (2009) **British Picture Vocabulary Scale (BPVS3)**, (3rd ed.). London: GL Assessment.
English vocabulary acquisition and understanding for 3 – 16 years.

Glutting, J., Adams, W. & Sheslow, D. (2000). **Wide Range Intelligence Test (WRIT)**. Florida, USA: Psychological Assessment Resources (PAR).
Underlying ability assessment for individual administration for ages 4 to 85.

Hulme C., Snowling M., Stothard SE., Clarke P., Bowyer-Crane C., Harrington A., Truelove E., & Nation K. (2009). **York Assessment of Reading for Comprehension (YARC)**.
London: GL Assessment.
One-to-one diagnostic reading assessment considering word recognition, reading fluency and reading comprehension for ages 4-16 years.

Messer, M.A. (2014). **Academic Achievement Battery (AABTM)**   Florida, USA: Psychological Assessment Resources (PAR).
Considers basic academic skills including basic reading, spelling, mathematical calculations and reading comprehension. For 4 – 85 years.

Reynolds, C. R. & Voress, J. K. (2007). **Test of Memory and Learning, (TOMAL2)**, (2nd ed). Austin, Texas, USA: Pro-Ed Inc.
Memory assessment battery for individual administration for ages 5 to 59:11.

Sheslow, D. & Adams, W. (2003) **Wide Range Assessment of Memory and Learning (WRAML2)**. (2nd ed.)   London: Pearson Education.
Considers individual's memory functioning. For ages 5 – 90 years.

Smith, A. (1982). **Symbol Digit Modalities Test (SDMT)**. Los Angeles: Western Psychological Services.
Considers information processing speed including attention, visual scanning, and motor speed. Use with caution as part of battery of assessment instruments. Ages 8 – Adult.

Torgesen, J. K., Wagner, R. K. & Rashotte, C. A. (2011). **Test of Word Reading Efficiency (TOWRE2)** 2nd Ed.   Austin, Texas, USA: Pro-Ed Inc.
Quick word reading assessment for individual assessment for ages 6 to 24:11.

Torgesen, J. K., Wagner, R. K., Rashotte, C. A. & Pearson, N.A. (1999). **Comprehensive Test of Phonological Processing (CTOPP2)**, (2nd ed). Austin, Texas, USA: Pro-Ed Inc.
Phonological skills for individual assessment for ages 4 to 24:11.

Wechsler, D. (2018). **Wechsler Individual Achievement Test (WIAT-III UK-T)**, (3rd UK Ed. for Teachers). London: Pearson Education.
Reading, language and numeracy assessment for ages 4 to 25:11.

Wilkinson, G. S. & Robertson, G. J. (2017). **Wide Range Assessment Test (WRAT5)**, (5th ed.). Florida, USA: Psychological Assessment Resources (PAR).
Reading, spelling and numeracy assessment for ages 5 to 85+.

APPENDIX 2

Teaching and Support Resources

Structured Literacy Programmes

Hornsby, B., Shear, F. & Pool, J., (2006) **Alpha to Omega Pack. Teacher's Handbook and Student's Book**. (6th ed). London: Heinemann. Also resources to support the programme. http://www.senbooks.co.uk/

Bald, J. (2007). **Using phonics to teach reading and spelling**. London: Sage.

Franks, E., Nicholson, M. & Stone, C. **Beat Dyslexia: a structured phonological approach covering early stages to full literacy**. Hyde: LDA. https://www.ldalearning.com/

Catch Up® Literacy One to one structured intervention for struggling readers - http://www.catchup.org/interventions/literacy.php

English Sounds Fun: For teaching children with specific learning difficulties who are learning English as a foreign language. ELT well http://www.englishsoundsfun.com

Combley, M. (Ed.) (2001) **Hickey Multisensory Language Course** (3rd ed): a structured multisensory teaching programme. London: Whurr. http://www.senbooks.co.uk/

Kelly, K & Phillips, S. (2016). **Teaching Literacy to Learners with Dyslexia**: a multisensory approach. (2nd ed). London: Sage. (Conquering Literacy Programme). http://www.senbooks.co.uk/

Letterland - phonics-based approach to teaching reading involving child-friendly mnemonic characters and stories to aid memory. http://www.letterland.com

Ellis, S, Ellis, T, Davison, J, and Davison, M (1999) **Lifeboat Read and Spell Scheme:**
A series of 10 books (100 photocopiable lessons).
https://www.robinswood.co.uk/series/lifeboat-read-and-spell

Nessy Reading and Spelling - works from the point the children are at.
https://www.nessy.com/uk/product/nessy-reading-spelling/

Orton-Gillingham Academy - American online program and resources.
https://ortongillinghamonlinetutor.com/

Reading

Several publishers offer a range of books to appeal to young people with low reading ability. The books are age appropriate and have a high interest level. This is a very small sample of what is available.

Barrington Stoke – Books offer high interest, low reading age books with a dyslexia-friendly font. http://www.barringtonstoke.co.uk

Dandelion Books and Magic Belt Series (phonic books and games) build on phonic knowledge (from age 3 to 14+). https://www.phonicbooks.co.uk

Pandora Books – range of reading and interest levels
https://www.pandorabooks.co.uk/

Raintree – range of reading and interest levels. https://www.raintree.co.uk

Rapid Reading - range of reading and interest levels.
http://www.pearsonschoolsandfecolleges.co.uk

Reading Rockets – suitable for a range of ages and levels. http://www.readingrockets.org

Rising Stars – Short fiction books for struggling readers. https://www.risingstars-uk.com

RM Books – ebooks. http://www.rm.com/products/rm-books

Cowling, K. & Cowling, H (1993) **Toe by Toe**. Baildon: Toe by Toe Publications.
https://www.toe-by-toe.co.uk

trugs – synthetic phonics teaching materials
Supports building phonic skills, vocabulary, spelling rules etc for use in schools and at home. Includes games for reinforcement of skills.
https://www.readsuccessfully.com/what-is-trugs

Units of Sound – personalised online reading and spelling programme
https://www.unitsofsound.com

English games to reinforce aspects of reading and writing
https://www.topmarks.co.uk/english-games/5-7-years/letters-and-sounds

Wolf Hill Series - range of reading and interest levels.
Oxford University Press. https://www.oupjapan.co.jp/en/products/list/1167

Wordshark 5
reinforces aspects of literacy and learning to read, write and spell
http://www.senbooks.co.uk/search/WordShark-5

Comprehension/Thinking/Inference

New Reading and Thinking (2000) and **More Reading and Thinking** (2016).
Wolverhampton: Learning Materials Ltd.

Spelling

Frohlich, C. (2010) **My Spelling Books 1 and 2**: High frequency and medium frequency words:
Sight words (I can spell). Frohlich Publishing
LOOK, COVER, WRITE and CHECK practical approach.

Stanton, L. (2016) **200 Tricky spellings in cartoons: Visual mnemonics for everyone.**
CreateSpace Independent Publishing Platform.

SEN Books (2009) **The Spelling Rulebook**. Wakefield: SEN Books.

Fletcher, H. & Caplan, M. (2014) **Anyone Can Spell it: A Guide for Teachers and Parents.**
Farnham: Helen Arkell Dyslexia Centre.

Raymond, S. **Spelling Tricks for Children**. Tamworth: Dragonfly Publications.

Rudling, J. (2015) **Spelling Rules Workbook**. How to Spell Publishing.

Spellzone: online spelling course - https://www.spellzone.com .

Spelling Window (Helen Arkell Dyslexia Centre)

Dictionaries

Maxwell, C & Rowlandson, J. (2012) **The school spelling dictionary**.
Edinburgh: Barrington Stoke.

Mosely, D. (2012) **The ACE Spelling Dictionary**. Hyde: LDA.

Writing

Colourful Stories – visual support to help structure stories
https://www.elklan.co.uk/under-5s/colourful-stories

Language enrichment and development - Black Sheep Press
https://www.blacksheeppress.co.uk/product-category/education/language-enrichment/

Graves, S. **Learning High Frequency Words** (2002). Wolverhampton: Learning Materials Ltd.

Nessy Writing Beach – considers punctuation, paragraphs, structure and story telling
https://www.nessy.com/uk/product/writing-beach/

Stowell, L. & Chisholm, J. **Write Your Own Story Book** (2011) Usborne Publishing
Ideas to promote writing and develop skills. https://usborne.com

Handwriting

Addy, Lois (2004) **Speed up! A kinaesthetic programme to develop fluent handwriting**
Hyde: Learning Development Aids (LDA).

Left handed writers
http://www.anythinglefthanded.co.uk

Pencil grips - Crossbow Education
http://www.crossboweducation.com/shop-now/handwriting-resources/pencil-grips?product_id=676

Triangular pencils from Zoro - https://www.zoro.co.uk

'Tramline' paper for handwriting – Hope Education
https://www.hope-education.co.uk

Mini Whiteboard/Dry Wipe boards and markers – Crossbow Education
http://www.crossboweducation.com/handwriting-resources/handwriting-resources-marker-boards

Stanton, Lidia (2017) **Which Way? Letter and Digit Reversals Workbook**
CreateSpace Independent Publishing

Touch Typing

Nessy Fingers - https://www.nessy.com/uk/product/nessy-fingers/

Dance Mat Typing - BBC Bitesize - Four levels of games to learn touch typing.
Available at http://www.bbc.co.uk/guides/z3c6tfr

Games

Topmarks – range of games and learning resources on various subjects
https://www.topmarks.co.uk

Learn Your Tables – reinforcement practice for multiplication tables
http://www.learnyourtables.co.uk/en/index.htm

SumsOnLine - mathematical activities
http://www.sums.co.uk

Osmo – 'hands on' games for ipad and iphone
https://www.playosmo.com/en-gb/

Numeracy & Maths - Structured Programmes & Support Resources

Beat Dyscalculia (Addacus) a structured multi-sensory numeracy programme
http://www.addacus.co.uk/index.php

Catchup ® Numeracy – one to one intervention and monitoring programme for learners who have fallen behind in numeracy - http://www.catchup.org/interventions/numeracy.php

Dynamo maths - Assessment and interventions for children with numeracy difficulties
http://dynamomaths.co.uk

Big Time Classroom Clock Kit, Learning Resources
https://www.learningresources.co.uk/product/big+time+learning+clocks+demonstration+clock.do?

Time Dominoes, Learning Resources
https://www.learningresources.co.uk/product/time-domino-game.do?

Numicon – multisensory resources and interactive whiteboard software
Oxford University Press - https://global.oup.com/education/?region=uk

Hit the Button - Timed quick fire games to reinforce aspects of numeracy
http://www.topmarks.co.uk/maths-games/hit-the-button

Numbershark 5 – reinforces various aspects of numeracy
http://www.senbooks.co.uk/view-product/Numbershark-4

Times Tables Snap - Green Board Games
https://www.funlearning.co.uk/product/learning/maths-games/times-tables-snap-cards/

Foreign Language Learning

Coffee Break Languages – podcasts can be downloaded in several languages.
https://radiolingua.com/

Duolingo – online learning and revision in several languages
https://www.duolingo.com/

Dyslexia and foreign language learning – inclusive practice website (Catriona Oates)
https://incpill.com/dyslexia/

Language Lizard

PENpal Audio Recorder Pen

http://www.LanguageLizard.com/PENpal

Penfriend

Software to help users to write faster and more accurately by predicting the next word.

Available in many languages.

http://www.penfriend.ltd.uk

Inspiration a mind-mapping program. A visual approach to learning

http://www.inspiration.com

International Dyslexia Association

Lots of information on dyslexia with information on training

http://www.interdys.org/

British Dyslexia Association

Lots of information on dyslexia with information on training and CPD for teachers

http://www.bdadyslexia.org.uk/

Clicker7

Tools for reading and writing French, Spanish-usually for younger learners

http://www.cricksoft.com/uk/products/clicker/home.aspx

Linkword Languages

Language learning through word association, multi-sensory language resources

http://linkwordlanguages.com

Linguascope

Resources for teaching languages – games and activities in a range of languages

https://www.linguascope.com

Etymological information online

Word information and morphology

https://www.etymonline.com/

Schneider, E. & Crombie, M. (2003). **Dyslexia and foreign language learning**.
London: David Fulton Publishers.

Multisensory Resources

Magnetic Rainbow Arc (for word building, vowels, consonants, spelling rules, rime and analogy, sequencing, phonics etc.) – Crossbow Education
http://www.crossboweducation.com/magnetic-rainbow-arc/shop-now/literacy-and-language/spelling-teaching-resources/spelling-teaching-resources-magnetic-resources

Wooden letters (lower and upper case) for forming teaching alphabet arc
http://www.crossboweducation.com/index.php?route=product/search&search=wooden

Mind mapping

Imindmap (Buzan) - https://imindmap.com

Inspiration and **Kidspiration** for planning and studying.
https://www.dyslexic.com

Mindfulness

Mind Up curriculum
https://mindup.org/mindup-mindful-classroom-framework-schools/

Assistive Technology

There is a huge range of material available and information is readily accessed through the internet. Sites such as http://www.dyscalculia.org/accessibility/ld-tools-software allow you to choose material for various aspects of dyslexia and dyscalculia. The main technology companies are now integrating assistive technologies and learning tools into their mainstream products. See for example, https://www.microsoft.com/en-us/Accessibility/ and https://ww.apple.com/accessibility/ You may have to be careful when choosing material and apps from American sites as spellings may vary. However UK sites such as BDA, CALL Scotland and AbilityNet UK also offer advice and recommendations. The following is a brief sample of some material which is available. Some of the programs could be under more than one heading but for convenience have only been included once.

Note taking
Notability – note taking and annotation - http://gingerlabs.com
OneNote - https://www.onenote.com

Predictive programs

Lightkey – works with Word to predict what learner wishes to say, cutting key strokes and reducing spelling errors. https://www.lightkey.io

Penfriend - http://www.inclusive.co.uk/penfriend-xl-4-1-p5025

Texthelp Read and Write - https://www.texthelp.com/en-gb/

Clicker 7 – literacy toolkit to help writing + reading and spelling
http://www.cricksoft.com/uk/clicker

Talking word processor

Write: Outloud – Talking word processor providing auditory output so student can hear as well as see what he is writing   http://assistivetech.sf.k12.sd.us/write_out_loud.htm

Text-to-Speech

Balabolka - http://www.cross-plus-a.com/balabolka.htm

Natural Reader - https://www.naturalreaders.com

WordTalk - http://www.wordtalk.org.uk/home/

Voice recognition

Voice Type - https://chrome.google.com/webstore/detail/voice-type-speech-to-text/mpmdkfliibnnpamgembpncenpjkmiddp?hl=en

Dragon NaturallySpeaking

https://www.nuance.com/en-gb/dragon/industry/education-solutions.html

Digital help with reading

C-Pen Reader – scanning pen that displays a word definition and reads text aloud to help support reading difficulties. An Exam Reader version is available which in some circumstances, can be used for examinations without the need for specific Access Arrangements.
http://www.readerpen.com

For Talking and Listening

Talking Tins encourage speaking and listening skills as well as writing and thinking. Uses include foreign language learning.

MyStudybar – mostly for older age group - range of free software for planning, reading, writing, vision and voice – available from Eduapps – further information and download from eduapps.org and from Call Scotland - http://www.callscotland.org.uk/home/.

Calibre Library

For children and young people struggling to learn to read, a selection of books is available for learners with dyslexia from Calibre Library.
https://www.calibre.org.uk

Voice activated intelligent personal assistants

Siri – for Apple devices
Alexa – Voice service connected by a speaker (e.g. Echo, Sonos One)

Digital Dictionaries

Franklin Collins English Dictionary with Thesaurus
Has phonic spell-correction which is helpful for those with dyslexia.

C-Pen Dictionary Pen
OCR technology which can look up words by passing the nib across the unknown word. The pen can display a definition and read the word.

Memory

Cogmed Working Memory Training – Pearson
http://www.pearsonclinical.co.uk/Cogmed/Cogmed-Working-Memory-Training.aspx

Mastering Memory – computer program and teaching manual
http://www.masteringmemory.co.uk

Study Skills

Cottrell, S. (2013). **The Study Skills Handbook** (Palgrave Study Skills) (4th ed.). Basingstoke: McMillan Publishers Ltd.

Godwin, J. (2012). **Studying with dyslexia** (Pocket Study Skills). Basingstoke: McMillan Publishers Ltd.

Thinking Skills

Bowkett, S. (2015). **100 Ideas for Primary Teachers: Developing Thinking Skills** London: Bloomsbury.

Useful Books and Online Resources for Teachers

Brooks, G. (2013) **What works for pupils with literacy difficulties? The effectiveness of intervention schemes** (4th ed.). London: The Dyslexia-SpLD Trust.

Buzan, T. (2005) Mind Maps for kids: An Introduction. London: Thorsons.

Buzan, T. (2004) Mind Maps for kids: Study Skills. London: Thorsons.

Buzan, T. (2011) Buzan's Study Skills: Mind Maps, Memory Techniques, Speed Reading and More! Harlow: BBC Active.

Buzan, T., Griffiths, C. & Harrison, J. (2013) Modern Mind mapping for smarter thinking. Cardiff: Proactive Press. (Available as an ebook)

Broomfield, H. & Combley, M. Overcoming Dyslexia 2nd Ed London: Whurr Publishers.

Brunswick, N. (2012) Dyslexia – A Beginner's Guide. Oxford: OneWorld Publications

Cochrane, K. Gregory, J. & Saunders, K. (Eds.) (2018) **The dyslexia friendly schools good practice guide** (2nd Ed.) British Dyslexia Association

Eide, B.L. & Eide, F.F. (2012) **The Dyslexic Advantage: Unlocking the Hidden Potential of the Dyslexic Brain**, New York: Plume Books.

Emerson, J. & Babtie, P. (2013) **The Dyscalculia Assessment** 2nd Edn. London: Bloomsbury Publishing Ltd.

Hornigold, J. (2015) **Dyscalculia Pocketbook**. Alresford: Teachers' Pocketbooks.

Jennings, P.A. (2015) **Mindfulness for teachers: Simple skills for peace and productivity in the classroom**. New York: W.W.Norton & Company Inc.

Jones, A. & Kindersley, K. (2013) **Dyslexia: Assessing and reporting – The PATOSS Guide**. London: Hodder Education

Kamil, M.L., Pearson, P.D., Moje, E.B. & Afflerbach, P.P. (2011) **Handbook of Reading Research**, Vol. 4. Abingdon: Routledge.

Mackay, N. (2012) **Removing dyslexia as a barrier to achievement**: The dyslexia friendly schools toolkit. Wakefield: SEN Marketing.

Ott, P. (2006) **Teaching children with dyslexia: A practical guide**. London: Routledge.

Pavey, B. (2007) **The dyslexia-friendly primary school**. London: Sage Publishing.

Reid, G. (2016) **Dyslexia – A Practitioner's handbook**, 5th Ed. Chichester: Wiley.

Reid, G. (2017) **Dyslexia and inclusion: Classroom approaches for assessment, teaching and learning**. London: Routledge.

Reid, G. & Green, S. (2016) **100 ideas for Primary Teachers: Supporting children with dyslexia**. London: Bloomsbury.

Reid, G. & Green, S. (2016) **100 ideas for Secondary Teachers: Supporting children with dyslexia**. London: Bloomsbury.

Stuart, M. & Stainthorp, R. (2015) **Reading development and teaching**. London: Sage.

West, T.G. (2009) **In the Mind's Eye: Creative Visual Thinkers, Gifted Dyslexics and the Rise of Visual Technologies**. 2nd Edn. Amherst NY: Prometheus Books.

Useful Websites

British Dyslexia Association - https://www.bdadyslexia.org.uk/

The Addressing Dyslexia Toolkit
A free resource for teachers, schools and local authorities on inclusive practice, literacy difficulties and dyslexia. Though funded by Scottish Government, resources and information have wider applications.
http://addressingdyslexia.org

The Dyslexia SpLD Trust is a collaborative website combining voluntary and community organisations with funding from the Department for Education to provide reliable information to parents, teachers, schools and the wider sector.
http://www.thedyslexia-spldtrust.org.uk

Phonics4free offers free lessons and games to promote phonics.
http://www.phonics4free.org

Beating Dyslexia. Written by people who are themselves dyslexic, the website offers advice and study programmes for all ages.
http://www.beatingdyslexia.com

CALL Scotland - http://www.callscotland.org.uk/home/

Dyslexia Scotland - http://dyslexiascotland.org.uk

International Dyslexia Association - https://dyslexiaida.org

LD Online - http://www.ldonline.org

Maths and numeracy difficulties - http://low-numeracy.ning.com

APPENDIX 3

Courses in SpLD for Teachers

This is a small sample of the courses available. In addition to dyslexia, some of the providers also run courses on dyscalculia. Training providers change from time to time and new providers come on-stream, so it is best to check what is on offer directly with the establishment.

Addressing Dyslexia Toolkit – online free resource designed for teachers, parents and young people in Scotland but available internationally to provide training and information – addressingdyslexia.org

Bath Spa University - https://www.bathspa.ac.uk/courses/pg-specific-learning-difficulties-dyslexia/

Birmingham, University of Birmingham - https://www.birmingham.ac.uk/postgraduate/courses/taught/edu/language-literacies-dyslexia.aspx

British Dyslexia Association - http://www.bdadyslexia.org.uk/educator/bda-services-educators

CALL Scotland run a range of short courses and webinars in supporting learners with dyslexia through the use of assistive technology - http://www.callscotland.org.uk/professional-learning/

Chester, University of Chester - https://www1.chester.ac.uk/study/postgraduate/dyslexia-research-and-practice/201809

Communicate-Ed - http://Communicate-ed.org.uk

Dublin City University - http://www.dcu.ie/courses/Postgraduate/institute_of_education/MEd-Specific-Learning-Difficulties-Dyslexia.shtml

Dyslexia Guild - https://dyslexiaaction.org.uk

Edge Hill University - https://www.edgehill.ac.uk/courses/spld-dyslexia/

Institute of Education, University of London - http://www.ucl.ac.uk/prospective-students/graduate/taught/degrees/specific-learning-difficulties-dyslexia-ma

Lancaster University – Dyslexia and foreign language teaching course - http://www.lancaster.ac.uk/study/free-courses/dyslexia-and-foreign-language-teaching/

Manchester, Manchester Metropolitan University - http://www2.mmu.ac.uk/study/postgraduate/taught/2018/16953/

Miles Dyslexia Centre, Bangor University of Wales - http://www.dyslexia.bangor.ac.uk/coursesforteachers.php.en

Oxford Brookes University - https://www.brookes.ac.uk/courses/postgraduate/pgcert-education-working-with-children-with-literacy-difficulties/

Real Group Ltd - http://realtraining.co.uk

South Wales, University of South Wales (Newport) - http://courses.southwales.ac.uk/courses/1280-postgraduate-diploma-sen-specific-learning-difficulties/

Stranmillis University College, Belfast - http://www.stran.ac.uk/informationabout/courses/senliteracy/medteachingchildrenwithspecificliteracydifficulties/

Wrexham Glyndŵr University - https://www.glyndwr.ac.uk/en/Postgraduatecourses/MAEducation/

APPENDIX 4

Glossary

Accommodations: a set of enabling arrangements which are put in place to ensure that the person with dyslexia can demonstrate their strengths and abilities, and show attainment.

APC (Assessment Practising Certificate): accreditation approved by British Dyslexia Association, the Professional Association of Teachers of Students with Specific Learning Difficulties (PATOSS) and Dyslexia Guild. This certificate gives approval that assessment and report writing meets the standard set by the SpLD Assessment Standards Committee (SASC).

Assistive technology: a device or tool that can help learners circumvent difficulties and improve their functional capabilities.

Audacity: free open source digital audio recording and editing software that can be used on almost any computer.

Base word: a word that has a meaning on its own to which affixes can be added to change the meaning.

Blend: a combination of letters to form sounds that make into words

Closed syllable: a syllable ending in a consonant. To teach closed syllables, with letter alphabet, lay out firstly open syllables such as ba, ca, da etc emphasising that because the vowel is open, it makes a long sound. Then add a consonant – bat, cat, dad showing the effect of closing the syllable so you get a short sound.

Consonant: a letter that is not a vowel; the sound made by a letter that is not a vowel. The sound is made by constricting the flow of air through the mouth.

Consonant blend: two or more consonants that are blended together – e.g. br, st, nd.

Consonant clusters: two or more consonants coming together. Children learn to blend these when sounding out or writing words – tr as in train, str as in stripe.

Confidence interval or band: the range of scores within which we can feel confident that the 'true' score lies. No test can be assumed to be 100% accurate all of the time and a margin of error has to be allowed for. Where confidence intervals are given in the report a 95% confidence interval is generally used. This means we can feel 95% confident that the 'true' score lies within the specified band or interval.

Criterion-referenced assessments: Tests or assessments that are designed to measure a learner's performance against a fixed set of expectations and criteria – for example the measurement of progress towards specific targets, the measurement of progress over a set period of time, measurement and recording of gaps in a student's knowledge, expectation that a pupil will be able to read a particular stage reading book at a predetermined age, expectation that a child will have certain knowledge of phonics at age 6.

CVC: Consonant-vowel-consonant.

Derivational morpheme: an affix that is added to a word to make a new word. It can make the word into a new part of speech or grammatical category - e.g. wonder, wonderful.

Digraph: two letters that make one sound. There are vowel digraphs (two vowels that make one sound) such as ai as in rain, and consonant digraphs (two consonants that make one sound such as sh as in ship.

Dominant hand: the preference of one hand over the other for fine and gross motor tasks. Though it is not a conscious choice, an individual's handedness usually is dominant by the time they come to school. Most people are right handed (90%) with approximately 10% being left-handed. However a few children will not establish a dominant hand and will be able to change between hands.

Grapheme: the written form of a phoneme e.g. igh saying /ī/.

Homophone: word which has the same pronunciation but different spelling and meaning.

Individual Education Plan/Individualised Educational Programme (IEP) (terms vary in different areas): a written plan aimed to help those with significant additional support needs. It details individualised strengths and needs, plans or programmes of teaching/support and those with responsibilities for implementation.

Kinaesthetic: pertaining to muscle sense and movement, by which weight, motion and position are perceived.

Language Master: a reading aid which consists of the Language Master audio recording and playback unit and specially produced audio cards with a strip of magnetic tape onto which a teacher can record. There is room on the card for a word, phrase or short sentence to be written along with a picture. The pupil plays the card through the unit to listen to the teacher's recording while at the same time reading the words. The pupil then records the words on the Student track and compares their reading to the teacher's. The pupil can play and record as often as necessary. This can be used for phonics practice and is particularly useful when learning a foreign language to give a good model while at the same time encouraging repeated practice till mastered.

Manipulatives: blocks or other material that will help solve mathematical problems.

Maths anxiety: negative emotional reaction and tension in the face of having to manipulate numbers or do mathematical calculations.

Meares-Irlen Syndrome (also known as Irlen Syndrome, Scotopic Sensitivity Syndrome or Visual Stress): Though there is professional debate about whether these are appropriate terms to use and whether they are the same disorder, the syndrome involves sensitivity to reading from contrasting print and background colours resulting in discomfort and a range of other symptoms which are unconducive to the development of reading. Signs of visual difficulty should be investigated by an optometrist to rule out any more serious problems.

Metacognition: understanding of our own thinking and reasoning processes, especially when engaged in learning.

Mnemonic: Device for committing something to memory.

Morphemes: The smallest meaningful unit of language that cannot be further divided.

Morphology: The study of how words are formed in language – how little parts of words (e.g. prefixes, suffixes) influence meaning. How morphemes are combined to form words and affect meaning.

Opaque (in relation to languages): a language that does not have a close correspondence between the graphemes and the phonemes.

Open syllable: a syllable ending with a vowel.

Orthography: how our understanding of letters and patterns of letters links to written words and accepted spellings.

Orthoptist: an allied health professional who is trained to diagnose and manage eye movement abnormalities.

Paired reading: a method of supporting reading by partnering two people together so they read aloud with fluency.

Partitioning: a method of working out maths problems by splitting large numbers into smaller units to make them easier to work with.

Pelmanism: Game that requires matching pairs - can be used to reinforce learning– for example, matching pictures with words. Can be easily adapted for various teaching points – for example spelling choices such as –oy or oi.

Percentile: refers to the percentage of persons in the standardisation group who score at or below a given score. For example, if someone's score is at the 98th percentile then they are scoring very high – in the top 2% of the population.

Phoneme: A perceptually distinguishable unit of sound. The smallest identifiable sound (e.g. sh is one sound (a phoneme) even though it is two letters).

Phonics: the method of teaching reading in which symbols correspond with sounds in alphabetic writing.

Phonology: the sound system of a language; relationships between sounds in a language or between languages.

Phonological awareness: refers to knowledge and understanding of the sound system of a language

Psychometric Tests – Tests used to assess a child's cognitive ability.

Reliability: the extent to which a test can be relied upon to produce the same (or almost the same) results in the same circumstances at repeated trials.

Root (root word) – a word or word part from which other words can be made, usually through adding prefixes and/or suffixes.

Semantics: Meaning or interpretation of meaning of words, sentences etc.

Sound-syllable association: understanding the relationship between sounds and symbols to decode and interpret language.

Special Educational Needs Co-ordinator (SENCo): Person responsible for a school's policy on additional support needs, sometimes referred to as Special Educational Needs (SEN).

SpLD Assessment Standards Committee (SASC): This body aims to support and advance standards in SpLD assessment, training and practice and encourage improvements in best practice in the assessment of specific learning difficulties. The SpLD Assessment Practising Certificate underpins these aims. See above. SASC has a responsibility for providing guidance on training and implementation of standards and for overseeing and approving processes of awarding SpLD Assessment Practising Certificates. http://sasc.org.uk.

SpLD Test Evaluation Committee (STEC): a subcommittee of the SpLD Assessment Standards Committee (SASC). It provides guidance and recommendations on assessment materials to SASC.

Standard score is derived from the raw score from a particular test. It enables comparison to be made with scores in different tests or with different people. It assumes a mean score of 100 as the average level that would be expected for the person's age. The following table shows descriptors commonly used in referring to scores in reports:

Score Range

Standard scores	Descriptors
131 or more	Very high
121 - 130	Well above average
116 – 120	Above average
111 – 115	High average
90 – 110	Mid-average
85 – 89	Low average
80 – 84	Below average
70 – 79	Well below average/Low
69 or less	Very low

From: Jones, A. & Kindersley, K. (2013) Dyslexia: Assessing and Reporting. The Patoss Guide. London: Hodder, pages 34-35.

Standard deviation: Scores around the mean of a distribution – how much a set of scores is spread around an average measure of variability. Deviations around the mean can be calculated to express as a standard deviation (variance).

Standardised test: Tests that have been administered with a large number of children, chosen to be representative of the population. They are used to compare a child with other children of the same age.

Stem (stem word): a word which forms the base of other words which are made by adding affixes – e.g. 'act' can form the base for words such as 'enact', 'actor', 'acts' etc.

Syntax: the principles that determine the order, sequence and function of words. How words work together to produce meaning in sentences.

Thinking skills: the mental processes we use to make sense of information, act on it, solve problems and create new ideas

Transparent (in relation to languages): a language that has close correspondence between the graphemes and the phonemes

Trigraph: three letters which together make one sound – e.g. igh saying /ī/.

Validity: the extent to which a test measures what it is intended to measure.

Visual stress: Visual stress (sometimes known as Meares-Irlen Syndrome or Irlen Syndrome): the feeling of unpleasant visual symptoms when reading, especially for a prolonged time causing distortion of print, illusions of the letters or words moving causing visual irritation. If there are symptoms, referral to an optometrist or other appropriately qualified professional eye specialist should rule out more serious problems of the eyes.

Vowel: Sound made by a letter which is pronounced with the mouth open. The letters a, e, i, o, u, and sometimes y are vowels.

Vowel digraph: Two vowels that together make one sound e.g. ai /ā/

APPENDIX 5

Forms and Contents of CD

The following pages contain examples of material that should be helpful in a classroom situation. Permission is granted to photocopy and/or download the originals from the enclosed CD and to adapt these for your own needs.

Word Documents on CD

Auditory Discrimination Checklist

Checklist for later Primary school and Secondary school

Early Primary school checklist

Example of a Writing Frame for use as model

Foreign language learning for the classroom Grid
    including blank proforma

Giving feedback to promote a growth mindset – 20 things we can do

Handwriting – Factors to consider that may indicate dyslexia

Lesson Plan proforma

Model of a Probe Sheet for key words

Pre-school checklist for dyslexia

Paired Reading – How to do it

Paired Reading – Record Sheet

Prompt Spelling – Guidelines for Practice

Prompt Spelling – Practice sheet

Suggested format for recording progress

Suggested format for recording the outcome of meetings and planning

CROMBIE - NURSERY / PRE-SCHOOL CHECKLIST
(for children in pre-school year)

	Possible Factor	Date Noted and Concerns	Action Taken	Follow up date Further Action or not?
1	Difficulty in reading a rhyme or playing rhyming games			
2	Lack of awareness of alliteration. E.g. the slimy snake slithered slowly …			
3	Difficulty in maintaining rhythm, clapping games, music, etc.			
4	Problems with sequential tasks such as doing up buttons.			
5	Difficulty in following and carrying out more than one instruction at a time.			
6	Clumsiness particularly when distracted.			
7	Slow speech development.			
8	Word finding difficulties.			

#		
9	Difficulty in repeating nonsense words especially if there are more than two syllables.	
10	Balance tasks such as repeating a rhyme whilst standing on one foot.	
11	Distractibility.	
12	Reaction speed slightly slower than peers.	
13	Visual perceptual difficulties.	
14	Auditory perceptual difficulties.	
15	Difficulty or slowness in automatising processes, e.g doing two tasks at same time.	
16	Family History.	
17	Other relevant factors to consider.	

Most of these signs will be present in ALL pre-school children to soem exent so take time to observe them. Steps can be taken to develop and encourage skills that a child finds difficult without the need to put in specail measures. An approach using games is often less stressful and using groups over a one-to-one setting helps to include children and give them a chance of achieving success in front of their peers. For suggestions of games see page XX.

CROMBIE - EARLY PRIMARY SCHOOL CHECKLIST

	Factor of Concern	Date Noted and Concerns	Action Taken	Follow up date Further Action or not?
1	Poor reading progress irrespective of approach used.			
2	Severe difficulty with spelling, sometimes using bizarre spellings.			
3	Condsiderable confusion over simple punctuation and grammar.			
4	Confusion of letters of similar shape, e.g. b/d p/q u/n f/t M/W.			
5	Omission or confusion of small words, the, a, so, to, of, for, etc.			
6	Auditory perceptual discrimination difficulties.			
7	Badly or wrongly formed letters.			
8	Uncertainty about when to use lower and upper case letters.			
9	Reversals of letters or whole words. e.g. 'was' for 'saw', 'god' for 'dog'			

10	Confusion of similar sounding letters. e.g. d/t, v/f/h, short vowels.				
11	Substitution of a word similar in meaning but with a different phonic pattern when reading.				
12	Faulty auditory sequencing in reading and in repetition of words: emeny for emeny, pasghetti for spaghetti.				
13	Foreshortening of words in written work intring for interesting.				
14	Difficulty in finding a name for an object.				
15	Difficulty in doing two or more things simultaneously, E.g skipping and reciting a rhyme.				
16	Transposals, e.g. sift for fist.				
17	Fusion of letters in words, e.g. our for our.				
18	Difficulty in remembering what day it is, address, phone number, etc.				
19	Difficulty in mastering sequence of days, hours, etc.				

#		Date Noted and Concerns	Action Taken	Follow up date Further Action or not?
20	Possible history of slow speech development.			
21	Difficulty in copying often worse from a distance such as from a screen or board.			
22	Difficulty or extreme tenseness in holding a pencil or pen.			
	In other areas			
23	Family history of reading and spelling problems.			
24	Difficulty in sequencing, days of week, etc.			
25	Confusion over directionality			
26	Difficulty in remembering short sequence of numbers, letters, etc.			
27	Mixed laterality.			
28	Difficulty in understanding temporal sequential concepts, e.g. yesterday, tomorrow, etc.			
29	Problems with simple mental arithmetic.			

30	Becomes emotionally upset when asked to read or write.		
31	Other relevant factors noted.		

Observation notes.

CROMBIE - SCHOOL CHECKLIST FOR LATER STAGES - (Late primary, middle or early secondary).

	Factor of Concern	Date Noted and Concerns	Action Taken	Follow up date Further Action or not?
1	Underlying ability and comprehension skills are at odds with reading and written work.			
2	Failing at reading with inability to cope with reading demands of curriculum without accommodation arrangements.			
3	Weak oral reading skills, inserting or omitting words, guessing, ignoring phrasing and punctuation.			
4	Avoidance of rading whenever possible, doesn't read for pleasure.			
5	Failure to spell adequately to allow reader to understand or barely comprehend meaning.			
6	Inconsistently in spelling even of previously memorised words.			
7	On-going confusion over spelling of homophones.			
8	Omission of letters or whole sylllables or addition of inappropriate ones when writing.			
9	Poor use of syntax and grammar.			

10	Mispronounciation, misuse or inability to accurately retain words for verbal use.		
11	Misunderstanding due to inadequacy of reading ability without accommodation. e.g. reading hysterical for historical.		
12	Difficulty in understanding and following sequences read aloud or in comprehending a sequence of directions.		
13	Difficulty in answering questions which rely on the interpretation of own written work.		
14	Difficulty in remembering the sequential movement patterns necessary for accurate letter formation, resulting in poor quality written work or presentations.		
15	Difficulty in remembering words and phrases which have been dictated.		
16	Reluctance to start writing tasks.		
In other areas			
17	Family history of reading and spelling problems.		

18	Extreme tenseness in holding a pen or pencil; or in starting writing on a computer.			
19	Note if there has been a recent hearing and/or a vision check and the nature of the check. Is there a need for any follow-up?			
20	Reluctance to go to school (may be reported by parents).			
21	Any other factors to note.			

Observation notes.

Auditory Discrimination Check

Tell me if these words are the same or different. *(The child should not watch your lips as you say them, so you may need to turn away or put a paper between you and the child so they can't visually determine the answer.)*

	Use natural speech and say the words with correct pronunciation. **Tick as appropriate**	**Discriminating**	**Same**	**Different**	**Notes**
1	word - sword	/w/ and /s/			
2	cat - cart	/t/ and /rt/			
3	same - fame	/s/ and /f/			
4	bin - din	/b/ and /d/			
5	line - line				
6	very - merry	/v/ and /m/			
7	fine - vine	/f/ and /v/			
8	merry - Mary	/ĕ/ and /ā/			
9	lamp - lamp				
10	ant - and	/t/ and /d/			
11	last - last				
12	sherry - cherry	/sh/ and /ch/			
13	better - wetter	/b/ and /w/			
14	waiver - waiter	/v/ and /t/			
15	range - range				
16	fair - there	/f/ and /th/			
17	met - meet	/ĕ/ and /ē/			
18	fan - fan				
19	under - wonder	added /w/			
20	Raith - rave	/th/ and /v/			

CROMBIE - CHECKLIST OF FACTORS WHICH MAY REVEAL DYSLEXIA.

	Factor of Concern	Severe Difficulty	Moderate Difficulty	Slight Difficulty
1	Underlying ability and comprehension skills are at odds with reading and written work.			
2	Failing at reading with inability to cope with reading demands of curriculum without accommodation arrangements.			
3	Weak oral reading skills, inserting or omitting words, guessing, ignoring phrasing and punctuation.			
4	Avoidance of rading whenever possible, doesn't read for pleasure.			
5	Failure to spell adequately to allow reader to understand or barely comprehend meaning.			
6	Inconsistently in spelling even of previously memorised words.			
7	On-going confusion over spelling of homophones.			
8	Omission of letters or whole sylllables or addition of inappropriate ones when writing.			
9	Poor use of syntax and grammar.			

10	Mispronounciation, misuse or inability to accurately retain words for verbal use.			
11	Misunderstanding due to inadequacy of reading ability without accommodation. e.g. reading hysterical for historical.			
12	Difficulty in understanding and following sequences read aloud or in comprehending a sequence of directions.			
13	Difficulty in answering questions which rely on the interpretation of own written work.			
14	Difficulty in remembering the sequential movement patterns necessary for accurate letter formation, resulting in poor quality written work or presentations.			
15	Difficulty in remembering words and phrases which have been dictated.			
16	Reluctance to start writing tasks.			
In other areas				
17	Family history of reading and spelling problems.			

Factors to consider in handwriting that may indicate dyslexia

Many of these factors will be seen in the writing of young children, so only consider these to be relevant in children from around the age of 7 or 8. It is unlikely that all of these factors will be evident in any one child with dyslexia.

	Severe Difficulty	Moderate Difficulty	Slight Difficulty	Comments
Reluctance to put information into writing.				
Difficulty in writing in sentences.				
Irregular spacing between words.				
Irregular spacing between letters, some merging.				
Handwriting not on lines if provided.				
Reversal of letters or numbers, e.g. 5 for s				
Reversal of whole words, e.g. was for saw				
Inversions				
Capital Letters at start of sentence				
Captial letters in usual places, e.g. Countries, Cities, etc.				
Sequencing errors - letters				
Sequencing errors - words				
Punctuation, use of full stops, commas, etc.				
Spelling - regular words				
Spelling - irregular words				
Awareness of phonic regularities, e.g. two 'o's say /oo/				
Signs of auditory discrimination difficulties, e.g. haf for have				
Uncertainty about directionality in starting writing letters				
Missing syllables, e.g. sist for sister				

Many of the factors mentioned are related to others in the list. However you should identify each factor even if these overlap – for example, 'Spelling' and 'Awareness of phonic regularities' inevitably overlap. The purpose of the list is to identify specific areas that require to be worked on. Identifying and recognising factors affecting a child's handwritten work will help you analyse difficulties and give points of focus. These can be worked on systematically in a variety of interesting ways using multisensory learning at a pace that will suit the individual.

CROMBIE - DYSLEXIA and LEARNING FOREIGN LANGUAGES.

Factors to take into Account Characteristics which may affect learning	Effect on FL Learning Learners may experience these difficulties	Approaches to Learning and Teaching	Additional Support
Phonological processing / Auditory perception • Poor grasp of sound/symbol correspondence • Lack of awareness of sounds within words • Unsure of sound which has been heard • Difficulty in perceiving the difference between similar sounds • Difficulty in knowing where a spoken word ends and the next begins	• Pronounciation, even of frequently encountered words • Recognition of familiar words and phrases • Confusion of similar sounding words • Reading especially if asked to read aloud • Knowing whether a sound is being pronounced correctly • Ability to recognise the difference between two words with similar sounds • Listening tasks • Answering oral questions	• Early introduction to phonic system of new language • Introduce new material in a multisensory way • Ask learner to read aloud only if s/he volunteers • Provide text to accompany sound • Exaggerate word separation, slow down speech at first, then speed up delivery later • Provide podcast for new vocabulary	• Use practice cards for reinforcement • Provide recorded material to accompany printed material • Use Language Master • Pair student with good reader • Don't ask learner to speak in large group • If learner has a choice of language, consider whether one with a similar phonic structure would be better • Consider complexity of language before choosing
Memory • Working memory is limited, if overloaded information maybe lost • May be inaccurate representations in long-term memory	• Remembering and following instructions • Remembering recently learned vocabulary • Repeating multi-syllable words • May know the answer but can't recall it	• Present new information in bite-size chunks • Set limited realistic targets • Make use of additional channels of learning • Allow extra time for recall	
Sequencing • Getting things in order, e.g. alphabet, word order in sentences, or letter order in words	• Accessing words from a dictionary or a list • Ordering days of week, months of year, etc.	• Provide frequent practice through a variety of approaches • Have lists diagrams, mindmaps on the wall for reference	• Make use of technical aids, computer, mobile phone, etc. • Encourage use of mnemonic approaches • Use visualisation strategies

Characteristic	Difficulties	Strategies
Writing • Handwriting can be painfully slow and the result inaccurate and difficult to read	• Copying • Committing spoken ideas to paper • Spelling may follow English phonic code	• Limit the amount of writing required for classwork • Avoid assessing written work if very poor • Accept assessment in forms other than writing • Provide photocopied notes with accompanying recording
Speed of processing • Tendency to be slower to respond to received information	• Responding to verbal instructions • Responding to continuous flow of information	• Slow down speed of presentation to allow extra time for processing • Be prepared to allow learner extra time to answer questions and complete work • Allow extra time in class and consider applying for access arrangements • Ensure class arrangements match exam arrangements
Difficulty with Directionality • Tendency to confuse left/right, up/down, etc.	• Following / giving directions • Responding accurately to instructions which rely on prepositions	• Provide pictures, arrows, etc. as well as text • Give visual clues when speaking • Pair student with one who has no difficulties in this area and who is happy to help
Grammar and syntax Inconsistently in spelling even of previously memorised words.	• Forming accurate sentences • Rules of grammar • Adjectival agreement • Word order esp. in complex sentences	• Teach rules and reinforce daily • Use diagrams, cards and other language building blocks to emphasise sequences and patterns • Write rules onto revision cards for learners as a reference tool
Visual discrimination, perception • Poor ability to discriminate or differentiate between words • Memory for recognising previuosly learned words • Visual stress, sensitivity to contrast in printed materials	• Differentiation between similar looking words • Differentiating between accents and assigning correct pronunciation • Confusion between languages, e.g. pain and bread (French/English)	• Use picture cues of association • Use practice cards for daily revision of common and irregular words • Highlight accents in colour • Use coloured paper for worksheets, etc. • Use Language master to aid learning of common words • Use highlighters and colour to emphasise various factors gender, word order, etc. • Mind-mapping and use of colour can be helpful
Emotional • Fatique • Low self esteem • Lack of concentration	• Poor effort • Lacking confidence to speak • Unable to sustain concentration losing track of conversation	• Show empathy • Buddy or pair with an understanding peer • Give regular prompts • Encourage learner to 'give it a go!' • Explain errors orally • Breal learning into small steps

CROMBIE - DYSLEXIA and LEARNING FOREIGN LANGUAGES   PLANNING GRID for schools.

Effects of dyslexia on foreign language learning	Specific areas of difficulty for our learners	Classroom Approaches	Support Approaches for use with Learning assistantts or at home

Approaches to help the learner with dyslexia

Paired Reading   (based on the work of Professor Keith Topping)

Paired reading is an effective way for parents, carers and others to help children with reading. It isn't the same as teaching reading so there is no danger of paired reading conflicting with classroom or specialist teaching. Children will not get mixed up, and they should enjoy the activities. Working with an older student is often very effective if that student has sufficient time and can empathise and follow the guidance.

The following guidance can be put into a leaflet for parents or older students to follow. There should however be an introductory meeting with a teacher to introduce the technique, ensure co-workers are happy that they know what to do, and to allow them to ask questions if they are unsure of anything.

What is needed?

Time

You require to set aside ten to fifteen minutes a day for the reading sessions. If you can only manage five minutes then this is better than no reading at all, but do make the effort to give at least ten minutes a day. Stop after fifteen minutes unless you are at a particularly exciting part of the story or the child really wants to continue a little bit longer. If doing paired reading at home, ensure the time chosen doesn't compete with the child's favourite television programme.

Books

A good selection of books is required so the young person can choose. It is better to read a real book at this stage rather than a digital download. What is most important is that the book should appeal to the learner. Don't worry if the book seems a little on the hard side. With this technique children can read more difficult books as they are supported throughout.

If the book has been read previously and the child wants to read it again, this is great. Hopefully the second reading will be better than the first and the child will remember at least some of the words not previously known, so the reading will be more fluent. However don't force the child to re-read a book again if they don't want to. It will not be enjoyed, and enjoyment is key to this process.

Place

Find a quiet place away from distractions. Children will not gain much benefit if they have to compete with television or the chatter of other children or family members.

Make sure both are seated comfortably and both can see the book clearly and easily and keep the place. Sit close together.

What to do

1. Show an interest in the book by chatting about it before starting. Talk about the picture on the cover, or the pictures at the beginning of the book. As you progress through the book, take a break at the end of a page or section and chat to the child about what they think might happen next, or anything that is appropriate to the story. Satisfy yourself that the child understands the main points of what is being read.

2. Start by reading aloud along with the child quite slowly so the child can keep the place. Try to read just a fraction of a second behind the child so you are aware of whether or not the child would have managed without help. Let the child set the pace, but don't allow the reading to be so slow that you lose the meaning of the words. It will help the child to follow if the adult or older child tracks along the text with their finger moving along at the appropriate pace. Track each word read carefully and ensure the child's eyes are following.

3. When the child gets a word wrong, come in immediately with the right word. The child then repeats the right word and the two keep on reading with a minimum of interruption to the flow. Don't let the child struggle and don't ask the child to sound anything out while using this technique. Gradually speed up the reading to a 'natural' reading pace.

4. When the child gets words right, smile and give words of encouragement. Let the child know you are pleased. Don't nag or fuss about the words that the child gets wrong.

Give constant encouragement throughout and praise frequently for good attempts and words pronounced or repeated correctly.

5. When you have been reading together for a little while, the child might want to try reading alone. Agree on a suitable sign for the child to use when ready (a nudge, a raised finger or a tap). This will avoid upsetting the flow of the reading. You then stop reading aloud and praise the child. Once the reader has signalled let the reader continue alone, but be ready.

Whenever the child starts to struggle for a few seconds or gets a word wrong, come in with the right word, and continue reading together as before. Make sure the child says the word correctly before continuing. When the child feels ready to read alone again, the same sign will tell you to be quiet, give praise and be ready to come in again as soon as there is any sign of difficulty. Try to finish reading at the end of a chapter so you can easily find the place when you start the next day.

Keeping a record

It is a help for the child, the helper and the class teacher to keep a record of what has been achieved together. Keep a note of what has been read each day. If the child is doing well or trying hard, write this down. A diary sheet is best. See example. This will let everyone in the process know at a glance just how well the child is doing. Let the child take the record in for the class teacher to see regularly.

If secondary school children get help from a support teacher, then it would be hoped that the extra encouragement would be provided. Everyone involved should be able to see what has been read, how the child is coping and be able to discuss stories in a positive way with the child.

Reading Record Sheet				
Name:		Class: S1	Week beg:	
Day	Book chosen	Time Spent	With Whom?	Comments
Mon				
Tues				
Wed				
Thurs				
Fri				
Sat				
Sun				
Teacher Comments:				
	Signed:		Date:	

LESSON PLAN PROFORMA

Name of Learner:		Date of lesson:		Length of Lesson:	
Long Term		**Objectives**		**Short term**	

Teaching Points	Timing	Activities	Resources	Comments

Learner evaluation
(metacognitive approach)

Tutor evaluation
(What needs to be tackled or changed for next time?)
Note: progress towards objectives)

Suggested format for recording progress

Progress Record (Literacy)					
Name:				Class:	
Dates	Reading (Book and page)	Phonics	Word Attack (Points covered)	Spelling	Notes

Columns can be adapted or changed to include Memory, Study skills or other relevant topics. Adaptations can also be made to the information recorded – spelling for example may contain the name of the book and page numbers or may be the points or word families. It is recommended that a separate sheet should be kept for Numeracy if this too requires individual or individualised work.

If progress is recorded regularly it can be kept brief and manageable. This allows for another tutor to take over in the event of teacher absence and the young person's learning should continue seamlessly.

It will further be helpful if the Progress Record Sheet details the approaches adopted. Columns will show the important areas to note – e.g. phonics, phonological awareness, essay structure or whatever is appropriate for the individual learner. Approaches might include for example, 'alphabet arc', visualisation, Simultaneous Oral Spelling (SOS), Onset and rime etc.

Dates	Reading approaches adopted	Spelling techniques	Word Attack approaches	Assistive technology	Notes

Suggested format for recording the outcome of meetings and planning.

Record of Meeting Form Date:

Name of School or logo

Nature of meeting: Initial/Review/IEP(details separately)/Transition
(Delete as appropriate)

Name: _____ DoB: _____ Class: _____

Those present and role:

Points of discussion:

Parental view: **Teacher view:**

Other:

Action points (include name of person responsible)

Date for next review:

I agree this is a accurate brief synopsis of meeting

Signatures:

Date:

Giving feedback to promote a growth mindset – 20 things we can do

1. Allow enough time for student to try different strategies but don't delay feedback for long.

2. Focus on effort and the way in which a task has been done – how could you have done this differently?

3. Consider previous efforts, but don't compare with classmates or siblings.

4. Use multimedia and multisensory methods. Whenever possible, show the learner different methods of getting to the answer.

5. Allow the student to explain how they solved a problem (even if they achieved the wrong answer).

6. Consider the approach used this time and discuss why it was or was not an effective way of getting to the answer.

7. Allow the learner to suggest how they might improve or do things differently.

8. Ensure praise is deserved, so focus on what was done correctly even if just a part of the task. False praise or over-praising lowers expectations.

9. Give clear and precise information.

10. Be empathic in your approach.

11. Be sensitive to privacy and the perception of others.

12. Give and maintain high expectations.

13. Don't criticise something the student is not expected to change next time or can't change next time.

14. Ensure that students understand that making errors is an effective part of learning.

15. Facilitate learning through giving guidance but not the answer – let the young person work out the answer from your feedback. Provide scaffolding.

16. Feedback should come in small enough pieces that the learner can act on points. Too much too soon will result in overload and the learner being overwhelmed.

17. Support written feedback with oral feedback.

18. Focus on strengths (what was right) and how to improve in a positive way.

19. Feedback should result in points for action.

20. Encourage getting work in before the deadline so there is time to change direction if necessary.